NOT MANY FATHERS

Developing Emerging Leaders Shoulder to Shoulder

Dr. Jonathan Ramsey, Jr.

Printed in the United States of America.

ISBN: 9798474155951

Table of Contents

ACKNOWLEDGMENTS

I first want to acknowledge my wife, the love of my life, Laverne Huberta Ramsey. She has traveled some rough and challenging roads with me during our ministry together. She has been my partner, my biggest supporter, my encourager, the one who prayed over me in the middle of the night when things looked bleak. I would also like to give special appreciation to my children, Ashley, Jonathan, and Nathan, who, along with my wife, have had to make many sacrifices for God to bring us to the many places that we have traversed together. In addition, more recently, my daughter-in-law Tamika Ramsey has now joined us on this journey.

Then I must say there would be no Jonathan Ramsey, Jr. without the spiritual parents God divinely chose to protect and nurture me in my years of development. My father and mother, the late Bishop Jonathan Ramsey, Sr., and Mother Evelyn Ramsey, placed their imprint on my life. I will forever be grateful for their love and support for me in the ministry throughout the years.

I also want to acknowledge my grandfather, John Alfred Ramsey, whom I never had the pleasure to meet. But his legacy and my father's legacy in ministry have been the impetus that has fueled my ambitions and drive and enabled me to accomplish many great things for the Kingdom.

My grandfather, the late Gonza Lee Twitty, was a strong and proud man who taught me the discipline of hard work and what it means to leave an inheritance to your children's children.

I acknowledge my father-in-law and my mother-in-law, the late Hubert and Lydia McKenzie, for their constant encouragement and support of my family.

Many thanks to the mentors, teachers, pastors, and -great leaders who have played a tremendous role in my life. Some of these people I speak about in the pages of this book have been models and examples of the characteristics of true spiritual parents.

I want to thank the many people who have allowed me to lead them as their pastor, administrator, and teacher. Many of these people have become pastors, teachers, and leaders in their own right.

Finally, I want to acknowledge the editor of this book, Brenda Tate, and Saibo Ndlovu, Sophia Walters, and Tiwanna Duncan Lewis, for providing the initial review of the content of this book. Also, I want to thank my daughter Ashley for formatting and publishing the book, Nathan Ramsey for branding and marketing, Jonathan and Tamika for oversight of the book cover and design.

FOREWORD BY DR. HUGH BAIR

Our future is not restricted or limited to a place called heaven; it is also found in future generations, a possibility we carry in our genes. We have an awesome, incredible biblical undertaking that is missional to prepare our sons and daughters to carry the baton of God's presence into future decades. If the Kingdom of God is to advance from generation to generation, there must be an intentional passing of the baton. This is what Bishop Ramsey is teaching us. In other words, our God is the God of Abraham, Isaac, and Jacob. The blessing of previous generations must be passed down to the next generation.

The younger generations thirst for connection, and they will do practically anything to get it. Technology has promised to satisfy that thirst, but it only produces the illusion of a promised connection without its deep fulfillment. They need fathers with whom they can connect and share their successes, struggles, dreams, and goals. They need fathers who will fan the gift of God into a flame and who will affirm them (2 Timothy 1:6). They need fathers prepared to put new wine into new wineskins to preserve it for future generations (Mark 2:22).

Bishop Ramsey, a scholarly practitioner in the field of mentoring and caring, writes from the pinnacle of wisdom that God has deposited into his heart. His procedure was first to discuss the issues, identifying the major points to be made. An example of this would be whether the way a person was fathered was damaging—due to the father's absence, abuse, or shaming. This book takes you through a step-by-step process to heal your father-wound by releasing unresolved abandonment. It is enormously useful because the sequences are a well-thought-out progression that you can use to release your potential. It gives a remarkable combination of diagnostic acumen and spiritual sensitivity that is rooted in the Bible. Additionally, it offers a wonderful balance of the theoretical and the practical side of mentorship, which is based on the depth and breadth of Bishop Ramsey's pastoral and diagnostic experience. This truth cannot be argued, only known through living and shared through the retelling of the experience.

Dr. Ramsey has become a father to many sons and daughters, and he is an excellent example. He gives a wide-lens experience of the manner in which he was mentored and his mentoring of others. Furthermore, he synthesizes a vast array of material that brings healing and provides clear direction and insight for everyone who needs to pass the baton and move the heritage of blessing forward to future generations. Bishop Ramsey is regarded by new and veteran pastors alike as a pastor of pastors and a father in the faith.

Dr. Hugh Bair holds a Ph.D. in Psychology and a Min. in Theology. He has served in the pastorate for over 30 years and is the Lead Pastor of Christian Life Church in Baltimore, Maryland. In his role as presiding Bishop of Christian Life Church, he also proclaims the Word through a radio broadcast and TV ministry.

PREFACE

Not Many Fathers

Too often, the value of someone or something is not realized until that person, or that thing is no longer accessible and can no longer be recovered. The loss of my father affirms this sentiment. I witnessed the physical effects of aging overtake my father; the frailty of his frame had become evident. However, his wit and mind remained sharp and intact. My father continued to speak great words of wisdom into my life, preparing me for the challenges that I would eventually face in my progression in ministry. As I walked in the door of the church for his memorial service, I came to the sudden and overwhelming realization of how much I would miss his voice, his touch, and his presence.

The need for a father's voice, a father's touch, and a father's presence are grossly apparent in the day in which we live. This is a pivotal point in history; the world faces alarming problems that have brought us to a global standstill. There is a growing need for spiritual parents who are equipped and committed to engaging this emerging generation that is desperately crying out for affirmation and guidance. This generation is struggling to find their identity, searching for spiritual role models they can follow, and many are battling feelings of abandonment and loneliness.

One day while sitting in my office, I received a phone call from a young man I had not seen nor heard from in over 20 years. I had met this young man while pastoring the second church in my pastorate. He recalled when he was removed from his family and entangled with the wrong crowd as we spoke. This young man had been reared in a home with high Christian values. But at the most turbulent period of his life, he had turned to drugs and alcohol. During this time, my father's example for me in ministry convinced me not to leave this young man in crisis. I resolved to go where he was. I found him in a heavy sweat, and he reeked of not having bathed in days. I prayed for his deliverance, and I committed to not leaving him in the same predicament I found him in.

During our call, he thanked me for saving his life. He stated that our encounter all those years ago at his lowest point changed the trajectory of his life. This young man is now a Youth Pastor at a church in New Orleans, Louisiana. He did not have a relationship with his biological father but felt that in me, he had found a spiritual father who cared for his soul. What my father had been for me, I seized an opportunity to duplicate in the life of someone else. That is what spiritual fathers do.

The Apostle Paul said though you might have ten thousand instructors in Christ, you do not have many fathers (1 Corinthians 4:15). There is a clarion call going out to all spiritual fathers to step forward and make the connections necessary to change the lives of this emerging generation forever.

-Dr. Jonathan Ramsey, Jr.

Introduction

It was a dream of a lifetime to be presented with the opportunity to speak at the 68th Annual General Assembly of the Church of God. As a young boy growing up in the Florida Cocoa offices of the Church of God, I never once imagined that I would be bestowed with such an honor. When the day came for me to speak, I woke up with butterflies in my stomach and was filled with anxiety. I flood myself with questions of self-doubt; "*what if I mistakenly said something that I should not say? What if I misspoke or mispronounced a word?*" However, more than anxious, I was humbled at the thought that the Executive Committee would choose me out of all my peers to be on the evening speakers. I realized what the weight and the depth of the opportunity truly meant. I would be standing on a platform in front of millions of people from all over the world. I knew that I could not stand alone. No, the moment was so much greater than that. I had to stand as a representative of something great and positive to come.

I was forced to reflect on the many people who had impacted my life and prepared me for such a momentous and life-changing experience. I thought about my State Administrative Bishop at the time, Bishop Quan L. Miller, who I had admired and attempted to pattern my life after for so many years. I thought of my former pastors, Bishop George Wallace, Bishop Thomas E. Chennault, and Bishop Walter D. Jackson, and of course my ultimate role model, my father, Jonathan Ramsey Sr., and the many lessons I learned from their examples.

Not only did I have great pastors who had made their mark on my life but also, in addition, I had to reflect on my former teacher, Mrs. Clapp, the person who took time to expose me to culture and a world that I had never experienced before. Another teacher is Mrs. Ellen Heidt, who told all of her students, *"you can become whatever you put your mind to being."* My college professors, Martin Baldree and Hubert Seals who helped me understand that ministry had to be a part of my spiritual DNA to be successful. Dr. Harold Hunter challenged my intellect to view the Word of God from a broader and more objective perspective.

That day, I rode around the city of St. Louis on a bus venturing back in my past to see the people who helped me get to where I was at that moment. During that ride, I could not help but think of how grateful I was that people took the time to invest in me.

I could not help but remember when I was 15-years-old when Marina Miller and Sister Mary Horne asked me to speak for five minutes on a Friday night at our Family Training Hour service. Who would have known that experience would be the starting point that would eventually place me on a platform with some of the most remarkable men the Church of God has ever witnessed? That night God tremendously used me to bless so many people's lives. Afterward, people spoke to me and told me how proud they were and how they had enjoyed the worship experience. My sermon topic that night was *"Ushering in the Glory Shoulder to Shoulder."*

That message spoke to the essence of my life—where God

had brought me from to where I was at the moment was not about Jonathan Ramsey, Jr. That moment was about the people who had poured so much of their life and energy into me to help me become the man of God I was. Today that becomes the impetus and motivation for this book entitled, *Not Many Fathers: Developing Emerging Leaders Shoulder to Shoulder.* The idea is that everyone who achieves anything significant needs others along the way to pursue God's purpose and plan for their life.

God strategically surrounds us with mentors and teachers who help develop the gifts that lie dormant in us. Every day of my life, I thank God that He counted me worthy to call me into the ministry. Along with that prayer is a prayer of thanksgiving for the many spiritual parents who loved me enough to take time with a young man who needed direction and discipline.

The Apostle Paul in 1 Corinthians 4:15 talks about spiritual parents who give birth to sons and daughters in the faith. *"For though you have ten thousand instructors in Christ, yet have not you many fathers: for in Christ have I begotten you through the gospel.*" This verse alone reveals to us a great opportunity we have in Christ to develop the emerging leaders, leaders who are waiting in anticipation for someone to show them their spiritual worth and pour life into who and what they can become.

Throughout the pages of this book, examples of men and women of God who sacrificed so much of themselves to help produce sons and daughters for the next generation. Today's leaders must move with the same resolve for there to be a radical and Godly change in a culture that is spiraling into an abyss of loss of identity, loss of self-worth, and loss of direction. If you are preparing to read this book, you must see yourself as a vital instrument of change in the hands of Almighty God to mold and shape the heart and minds of those God has placed in your care.

I will never forget the story a young man shared with me when I had gone back to preach at a conference at the Cathedral Church of God in Deerfield Beach, FL, where I had formerly pastored. The young man asked me the question, "*do you remember the day that you walked out of the office of the church and began to talk to three young men who were strung out on drugs and struggling to make it to their destination?*" I honestly had to tell him that I could not recall that day. However, he went on to share with me that he was one of those young men. He distinctly remembered me praying for them and telling them I would be there for them if they ever needed me. That young man eventually became a member of the church and the leader of the Men's Ministry years later. All I could think of at that moment was, *what if I had failed to hear the voice of God in that hour beckoning me to move outside of my comfort zone of the four walls*? I would have missed a divine opportunity to be instrumental in radically reshaping that young man's life.

Famous Psychologist Dr. Shane Lopez said, "*The tiny ripple of hope you set in motion can change the path of someone's life.*" That statement became a reality in Bobby's life. You, too, can make a difference in some person's life even if their life is floundering out of control when they are brought into your view. Perhaps you are the spiritual parent they have been praying for all of their life. Shoulder to shoulder, let's step forward and be that mentor, teacher, and spiritual parent who will make a difference.

- Dr. Jonathan Ramsey, Jr.

Endorsements

"*Not Many Fathers*" is a compelling call to nurture our sons and daughters in the things of God. A personal friend and esteemed colleague in ministry, I can highly recommend Dr. Jonathan Ramsey's book. It is both a "why" and "how" discourse that motivates us to "make up the hedge and fill in the gap" for young people who need a spiritual father…so many who are searching for answers and direction. The book is a scripturally based and culturally relevant study for parents, pastors, teachers, teens, and young adults. And I recommend it also as a timely impact study for the entire church family.

- *Bishop J. David Stephens, 2nd Assistant General Overseer*

This is a powerful book. When leaders, mentors, and heroes are sought, we need fathers. There is something special and devout about fathers, and Jonathan Ramsey has captured it. Through biblical insights and stories, a thoughtful and relevant lens is provided for the Church today. The voice, the presence, and the love of the Father are presented. Going further into the community, the impact, and the sacrifice of God the Father, each chapter lays out a path for a fatherless generation to follow.

The tragedy of the absence of fathers is well documented in this book. And it is matched and exceeded by the reality carefully and thoughtfully chronicled in this book; that fathering a rising generation is still possible now and for eternity.

-Oliver McMahan (Ph.D., Georgia State University; DMin, Brite Divinity School) is Vice President for Institutional Effectiveness & Accreditation and Professor of Clinical Mental Health Counseling at Pentecostal Theological Seminary in Cleveland, Tennessee, USA.

The author, a respected leader of the Church of God, made me "walk" through valuable and instructive pages of his academic work—showing the importance of spiritual parents, like the prophet and man of God, Elijah (spiritual father to Elisha).

My friend, Dr. Jonathan Ramsey Jr., is not just another person with international experience. He is a pastor of souls, highly committed to the ministry. My family personally had the opportunity to experience his care and guidance during some of the most crucial moments of our lives. Those who will read this book will be challenged and blessed as so many have been in the past across Florida, Southern New England, and globally.

With all the competence, knowledge, and experience accumulated throughout the years, it is time for his writing skills to be exposed and shine. And I cannot stress it enough; his message will reach places he will probably never visit in person.

This book will help you understand how important it is that we have spiritual parenting models like Elijah was to Elisha and the importance of Paul in Timothy's and Titus' lives. Bishop Ramsey also speaks to the need for this type of mentorship to be continued today with the many emerging leaders of this generation.

I highly recommend and endorse Bishop Ramsey's work.

-Carlos Boaventura, Ph.D., is a Professor, Writer, and Director for Dardah University for speaking Portuguese countries.

Bishop Asbury R. Sellers

I count it an honor to recommend *Not Many Fathers* to you as a source of inspiration and knowledge. This book is a real eye-opener for those in need of spiritual fatherhood as it is filled with examples and instances. Bishop Ramsey is a tremendous pulpiteer and orator of the Gospel and his compassion for spiritual fathers to come alongside young men and women and nurture them is evident throughout the book. Spiritual fathers are to discipline caringly while helping young people feel strong enough to handle life's circumstances. Read this book—and you will learn from one of the best.

-Bishop Asbury R. Sellers – Harvest Ministries

Bishop Raymond Hall and Dr. Arlene Hall

Not Many Fathers: Developing Emerging Leaders Shoulder to Shoulder addresses the leadership gap of our time. This concept of *Not Many Fathers* is as relevant today as it was in the Apostle Paul's time. This book speaks not only to the leadership need in society today but especially to the leadership gap in the **Body of Christ.** Ramsey makes the case that spiritual fathers are essential for molding, maturing, and shaping the trajectory of spiritual daughters and sons in the kingdom of God. He has demonstrated through Scripture and experiential knowledge that spiritual fathers can transform and shape the lives of sons and daughters. Eli was able to directly impact Samuel, a young leader, far beyond the way he was able to **influence** his sons (1 Samuel 3:9).

Bishop Ramsey has been a spiritual father to both of us, Bishop Raymond Hall and Dr. Arlene Hall, and continues to be very influential in our lives. He was our "Jethro" who showed up just when we needed to hear, *"You are not able to do ministry alone"* (Exodus 18:18). He was our "Mordecai" who boldly declared to us, *"For if you keep silent … who knows whether you have come to the kingdom for such a time as this"* (Esther 4:14). His voice resonates even now. Today we are both serving as pastors shoulder to shoulder because of the impact and impartation of Bishop Jonathan Ramsey.

We believe this book will change your perception of spiritual leadership regardless of where you are on the continuum of your leadership journey. Whether you are a "Jethro" or a "Moses;" whether you are a "Mordecai" or an "Esther." You are standing on someone's shoulders, and you need to be a shoulder for emerging leaders.

-Bishop Raymond Hall and Dr. Arlene Hall are Founding Pastors of Deliverance Temple Worship Center in Boston, Massachusetts.

Chapter 1

Not Many Fathers

The culture we live in directly challenges the traditions bestowed upon us by older generations. Teachings given to us as truths by our parents are now considered antiquated and out of touch with the current reality. However, let's examine the principles that were imparted to us in the past. We can discover that they were safeguards against life's dangers and snares that could ultimately destroy our future. The world around us is daily becoming more the antithesis of righteousness, godliness, and purity. We now live in a world of *political correctness*, tolerance and are consumed with a spirit of relativism without any sense of values, standards, or honor for God and His Word.

Today, it is all too common to hear sarcastic and belittling jokes that target the Church, preachers, and people who attempt to be faithful to God and His Word. Churches today are being judged in the court of public opinion, and those who profess their love for God are looked at and received strangely. They are targeted for retribution and are even being ostracized. In this hostile environment, this generation is being forced to navigate and build lives for themselves and their families.

As there is indeed nothing new under the sun, the culture we now live in is much like the culture and the times of the Apostle Paul. It is in direct response to these times that Paul was moved to write to the Corinthian church about spiritual fatherhood.

Corinth had an estimated 100,000-600,000 people; it was the main port for commerce and merchants. It was a booming city made up of permanent residents of many nationalities. The people of Corinth were affluent, having experienced great prosperity and success. Sexual immorality was rampant, and the youth of that day were prey to abuse and promiscuity. Corinth had developed weak social norms and a high tolerance for deviant behavior. They had statues that were 1800 feet high that were sensual in nature. They had a temple of Aphrodite, which symbolized the lust and corruptness of the people (Munn, G.L., 1960).

In this type of culture, Paul established the church of Corinth on his second missionary journey. Much of the corruptness of the culture had begun to creep into the Church. Rather than the Church making an impact on the culture, the Church was becoming seduced and enthralled by what was taking place at the time. For this reason, Paul writes this letter to the Corinthian church reprimanding them for their pride, deviance, and arrogance. Paul identified the need for spiritual fathers who would give guidance and leadership to a young but growing church.

Paul said you have ten thousand teachers or instructors, but you only have one spiritual father (1 Corinthians 4:15). The word instructor is from the Greek word, *paidagogoi,* which means a guardian or slave guide. This was the person who escorted the boys to and from school. They had the responsibility of supervising their general conduct. The word paidagogos referred to a slave who had special responsibility for a boy. *"The paidagogos was the personal attendant who accompanied the boy, took him to school and home again, heard him recite his lines, taught him good manners, and generally looked after him; he was entitled to respect and normally received it"* (Morris, 1985). What distinguished an instructor from a father was that the instructor did not have legitimate authority like a father, so the students did not necessarily respond to the instructor's instructions as sons would (Brown, 1871).

Today, teachers and administrators are tasked with enforcing school policy. However, at times, students may not be receptive and may seek to challenge those policies. School professionals are limited in their abilities to redirect students because though they may have authority, it is limited, unlike that of a father. Paul likens this to the Church; he says you have many persons giving you instructions of how you should conduct yourself, but you only have one spiritual father who has begotten you in Christ. Paul was conveying that many people attempt to exercise spiritual authority over your life. But the problem with those individual's exercise of authority is that their power is not legitimate. However, Paul gave direction and leadership to the Church from a position of legitimate apostolic authority. Paul could say, I established you in the faith, and based on that fact, I have the spiritual right to say the things I am imparting to you.

In 1 Corinthians 4:14, as a spiritual father who cares for his spiritual sons and daughters, Paul says I don't admonish you to embarrass you or make you seem small, but it comes out of genuine love and affection for you. Paul felt the need to remind the Corinthians of their responsibilities as Believers. Paul called them his beloved sons. Attributing this title to them reveals the care and compassion he felt toward them.

When I was growing up, there were times that I would make poor choices that my father would find highly disappointed. In those times, my father would sternly yet lovingly both correct me and affirm his unconditional love for me as his son. This was the message Paul conveyed to the Corinthian saints.

God uses us as instruments of His divine purpose to win people to Christ, but Paul says this does not give us the right to dictate their lives from a place of apostolic authority. However, we need spiritual fathers who will give birth to spiritual children and nurture them in the things of God to prepare them for the journey ahead.

Paul's issue in his day is still a challenge for both church leaders and congregants alike. On the one hand, people in leadership must know how to be in a position of authority but at the same time function from a place of humility and compassion. Peter puts this in perspective when he provides a path every leader should follow:

1 Peter 5:3 *"Neither as being lords over God's heritage but being examples to the flock"* (KJV, 1998).

Peter knew this from firsthand experience of watching Jesus' model of leadership. Jesus taught from a position of authority, but

He demonstrated great strength in the posture of servanthood. The greatest example of this is when as Jesus is preparing for His death, He arises from supper with the disciples and begins to wash the disciples' feet. Jesus reprimanded John and Andrew when they, along with their mother, approached Him with the request that her two sons be placed on the right and the left of Jesus when they come into His kingdom. Jesus responded sharply to that request stating that this is the practice of the Gentiles, to lord over those who serve them. But Jesus said that whoever wishes to be great let him first be a servant (Matthew 20:27; KJV, 1998; Maxwell, 2018).

Leaders must be sensitive to the fact that they are not perceived as attempting to control the lives of the people they oversee through the practice of manipulation or abuse of power because of their positions. At the same time, those persons they lead must carry a high level of respect and honor for those God has placed over them in the Lord.

In his book, Developing the Leader Within You 2.0, John C. Maxwell gives five levels of a leadership model. This model demonstrates leadership from the lowest level, which is positional leader, to the highest possible level of leadership, which is called the pinnacle. He said few leaders ever attain the highest level because it requires an example of years of self-sacrifice and dedication. But he also says everyone who is given a position of authority can achieve the first level of positional leader (Maxwell, 2018).

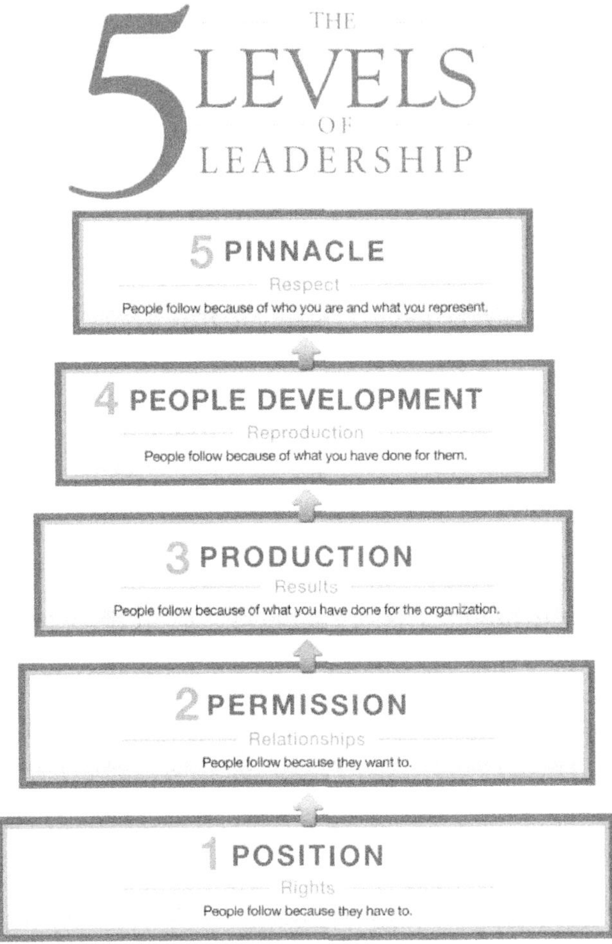

John Maxwell further states, *"People who have been appointed to a position may have authority, but that authority doesn't exceed their job description. Positional leaders have certain rights. They have the right to enforce the rules. They have the right to tell people to do their jobs. They have the right to use whatever power they have been granted"* (Maxwell, 2018).

But authentic leadership is more than having granted

authority. Real leadership is being a person other people will gladly and confidently follow. *"Real leaders know the difference between position and influence"* (Maxwell, 2018).

My life experiences have allowed me to witness leadership displayed in both the secular and church arenas. There have been times when I have been able to celebrate the gift of leadership demonstrated by great spiritual fathers who carried out their responsibilities with dignity and honor. However, there have also been times when I have seen leaders who did not understand their role in that capacity nor their commitment to God, which accompanied it. These leaders who abused their power to achieve their agendas fell short of what Paul described when he wrote to the Corinthians. I have seen the spirit of exploitation and manipulation in its darkest form—even to the point where people felt they could not eat, drink, or sleep without the permission of their leader. This is what Paul was warning against. Paul admonished spiritual fathers to act in the best interest of those they are commissioned to.

I am reminded of Bishop Bill Sheeks, former Third Assistant of the Church of God. He was a man who carried great respect because he had amassed much wisdom through many years of experience. He was beloved by many because he showed compassion and grace *even* when he was called upon to give correction and discipline.

On many occasions, I can remember calling him to seek out counsel regarding critical situations I had to tend to; one case stands out. If not handled properly, this situation had the potential to be highly explosive. In that call, Bishop Sheeks operated as a spiritual father. He prayed with me and offered guidance concerning the matter. As a result, I left the call feeling empowered, assured, and able to navigate the situation. Even after Bishop Sheeks was no longer my liaison, he would call me to check up on me—there was a relationship beyond the position.

Let us observe how Paul carried out his responsibility of being a spiritual father. Like a natural father, Paul provided discipline and correction, but his discipline came from the revelation that God had given him. Paul taught and trained the people to obey God's commandments and code of behavior given to us by the Word of God. Paul led by example. He suffered a personal loss to become a role model, revealing to people the discipline necessary to be a child of God.

Why was it necessary that Paul start with discipline in teaching the saints? Discipline and correction share boundaries for life situations. Discipline provides safeguards and protection. Discipline provides structure and order. Roy L. Smith said, *"Discipline is the refining fire by which talent becomes ability"* (Young, n.d.).

The book of Proverbs gives many scriptural applications of the benefits of discipline:

> Proverbs 15:32: *He that refuseth instruction despiseth his own soul: but he that heareth reproof getteth understanding* (KJV, 1998).

Proverbs 23:22: *Listen to your father who begot you, And do not despise your mother when she is old* (KJV, 1998).

Proverbs 1:8: *Hear, my son, your father's instruction and do not forsake your mother's teaching* (KJV, 1998).

Proverbs 3:11-12: *My son, despise not the chastening of the Lord or loathe His reproof. Even as a father corrects the son in whom he delights* (KJV, 1998).

The second thing Paul exemplifies in his model of spiritual fatherhood is guidance and direction. He does this through the impartation of wisdom, encouragement (*even in rebuke*), and mentorship.

Mentorship is a relationship between two people where the individual with more experience, knowledge, and connections can share what they have learned with a junior individual within a certain field (Oshinkale, 2019). The more senior individual is the mentor, and the junior individual is the mentee. Mentorship is the guidance provided by a mentor, especially an experienced person in a company or educational institution. Paul exemplified this practice by the many ways he poured his life into others through training and empowerment.

The primary purpose of a mentor is to lend their knowledge and experience to help a mentee realize their fullest potential. Here are five ways in which Paul encouraged others to maximize their potential in Christ:

1. Mentors empower people to make positive choices (Wood, 2016). Paul instructed the Galatian saints to submit their lives to Christ and deny their worldly passions and desires. In so doing, their choices and decisions were directly inspired by the Holy Spirit (KJV, 1998).

   Galatians 5:24-25, ESV: *"And those who belong to Christ Jesus have crucified the flesh with its passions and desires. If we live by the Spirit, let us also keep in step with the Spirit."*

2. Mentors encourage people to take ownership of their learning (Wood, 2016). Paul instructs Timothy to prepare himself through study and the discipline of reading God's Word.

   2 Timothy 2:15: "*Study to show thyself approved unto God, a workman who needeth not to be ashamed, rightly dividing the word of truth*" (KJV, 1998).

3. Mentors encourage people to develop the life skill of endurance (Wood, 2016). Paul admonishes ministers to understand that the race we are in must be accomplished by living a life of discipline and self-denial.

   1 Corinthians 9:24-27: "*Know ye not that they which run in a race run all, but one receiveth the prize? So run, that ye may obtain. And every man that striveth for the mastery is temperate in all things. Now they do it to obtain a corruptible crown; but we an*

incorruptible. I therefore so run, not as uncertainly; so, fight I, not as one that beateth the air: But I keep under my body, and bring it into subjection: lest that by any means, when I have preached to others, I myself should be a castaway" (KJV, 1998).

4. Mentorship helps people develop core values (Wood, 2016). Paul tells us that at the core of who we are is the depth of how much we are willing to surrender the lifestyle of the old man to the Lordship of Jesus Christ. This alone will allow us to walk in righteousness and true holiness.

   Ephesians 4:22-24: *"That ye put off concerning the former conversation the old man, which is corrupt according to the deceitful lusts; And be renewed in the spirit of your mind; And that ye put on the new man, which after God is created in righteousness and true holiness"* (KJV, 1998).

5. Mentorship strengthens interpersonal skills and peer relationships (Wood, 2016). In Colossians 4:7-18, Paul provides a listing of different people serving in different levels of the Church.

   Colossians 4:7-18: "*All my state shall Tychicus declare unto you, who is a beloved brother, and a faithful minister and fellow servant in the Lord: Whom I have sent unto you for the same purpose, that he might know your estate, and comfort your hearts; With Onesimus, a faithful and beloved brother, who is one of you. They shall make known unto you all things which are done here.*

> *Aristarchus my fellow prisoner saluteth you, and Marcus, sister's son to Barnabas, (touching whom ye received commandments: if he come unto you, receive him;) And Jesus, which is called Justus, who are of the circumcision. These only are my fellow workers unto the kingdom of God, which have been a comfort unto me. Epaphras, who is one of you, a servant of Christ, saluteth you, always labouring fervently for you in prayers, that ye may stand perfect and complete in all the will of God. For I bear him record, that he hath a great zeal for you, and them that are in Laodicea, and them in Hierapolis. Luke, the beloved physician, and Demas, greet you. Salute the brethren which are in Laodicea, and Nymphas, and the church which is in his house. And when this epistle is read among you, cause that it be read also in the church of the Laodiceans; and that ye likewise read the epistle from Laodicea. And say to Archippus, Take heed to the ministry which thou hast received in the Lord, that thou fulfil it. The salutation by the hand of me Paul. Remember my bonds. Grace be with you. Amen"* (KJV, 1998).

Paul outlines the importance of them understanding their interrelatedness and the need to provide care, help, and support for each other. Paul shows the tenderness and the character of a spiritual father in the words he uses in his greetings to his spiritual children in these verses.

In speaking of Onesimus and Tychicus, he calls them beloved brothers (1 Colossians 4:7-9). Paul uses words like a fellow prisoner, fellow servant, and fellow worker when sending a message to people he was giving guidance to, encouraging them that they were not in this alone. Paul was in partnership with those who served with him in the ministry. Paul could bring the principles of mentorship together with spiritual fatherhood and produce capable spiritual children in the Gospel.

Though mentorship does not equate to spiritual fatherhood, spiritual fatherhood must have a vital component of mentorship. In unpacking Paul's model of spiritual fatherhood, no relationship so highlights this more than how Paul spoke of Timothy in terms of sonship. We observe in 1 Timothy 1:2 how Paul refers to Timothy as his son. Paul used this term twice in the same chapter. We know through other references in Scripture that Timothy was not Paul's biological son. Still, the relationship he shared with him went beyond mentorship to one of a father-son bond.

> 1 Timothy 1:2: *"Unto Timothy, my own son in the faith: Grace, mercy, and peace, from God our Father and Jesus Christ our Lord"* (KJV, 1998).

> 1 Timothy 1: 18: *"This charge I commit unto thee, son Timothy, according to the prophecies which went before on thee, that thou by them mightest war a good warfare"* (KJV, 1998).

Acts 16:1-3 provides more context into Timothy's background. It indicates that Timothy was already a Christian when Paul first met him in Derbe and Lystra. Paul's relationship with Timothy is a clear example of the terminology of spiritual fatherhood. When we look at Philippians 2:19-23 and 2 Timothy 1:1-5, we see how Timothy clung to Paul as an apprentice would to his master teacher. In Philippians 2:22, Paul speaks of Timothy serving with him in faithful service like a child serving with his father:

> *"But ye know the proof of him, that, as a son with the father, he hath served with me in the gospel"* (KJV, 1998).

In 2 Timothy 1:5, Paul says, *"I am mindful of the sincere faith within you, which first dwelt in your grandmother Lois and your mother Eunice and am sure that it is in you as well"* (KJV, 1998). What a powerful commendation of what Paul has seen in his time of ministry with Timothy; one of commitment, one of loyalty, and one of a unique kinship in Christ. Paul not only made the call for leaders to become spiritual fathers but provided a blueprint through his example.

The continual cry of sons and daughters seeking affirmation and support from spiritual fathers confirms the critical need for church leaders who will pour into the next generation. Author and Pastor Jake Kail describe four characteristics of spiritual fathers. These characteristics exemplify the practice of spiritual fatherhood and are essentials that are necessary for today.

First, he speaks on having a heartfelt connection with those you father in the spirit. There must be a bond that allows the spiritual father to have the permission to minister to the hurts and the pains of those he invests his life into.

Secondly, there must be consistency in prayer for those we

desire to father. This generation is in dire need of prayers from those who have blazed the trail before them because they understand the pitfalls and the snares that await those coming behind them.

Thirdly, there must be an impartation. As Elijah imparted an anointing into Elisha's life, as Moses imparted wisdom and instruction into Joshua, as Jacob imparted blessings onto the life of his sons, so must there be a spiritual impartation into the lives of sons and daughters.

Finally, what would sons and daughters do without having someone to come alongside them and encourage them? No matter how well prepared the person might be for ministry, at some point, they will be confronted with challenging circumstances. In these moments, we need someone to help us cross the bridge of doubts and fears to a sense of renewed faith and assurance (Kail, 2015).

The leadership model Paul provided in the life of young Timothy must be duplicated through the lives of spiritual fathers in this hour. Without this demonstration of care and support for spiritual sons and daughters, they are left to face the challenges of ministry alone.

In *The 21 Irrefutable Laws of Leadership*, John Maxwell shares the following statistics: "*10 percent of those leaders were leaders because of natural giftings, five percent of them as a result of crisis, and 85 percent because of the influence of another leader*" (Maxwell, 1998). This analysis draws a connection that validates the importance of spiritual fathers in the lives of spiritual sons and daughters.

I distinctly remember one occasion when I was faced with a crisis in the region where I was the supervisor. As I was writing this book, I was notified that a man who had served as a spiritual father to many sons had passed away. Although he had attained the highest levels of leadership in his denomination, he never lost heart and compassion of a father. While I was frantic and perplexed about what the outcome might be, he, Paul Laverne Walker, like a gentle, wise father, spoke with profound wisdom and truth that helped me resolve the matter. As a result, what could have taken years to untangle only took a matter of hours.

As I reflected over my ministry at the time of his death, I began to write down the names of some of the men who had been spiritual "Pauls" in my life. I realized how much I needed to thank God for strategically placing them in my life during critical junctures of my ministry.

Philippians 3:17 reads, *"Brethren, be followers together of me, and mark them which walk so as ye have us for an ensample"* (KJV, 1998). Paul's suffering, endurance, love for the saints, commitment to the faith, and perseverance under duress demonstrated that he was willing to give of himself to see others be successful sacrificially. Paul became an example of everything he was calling upon others to fulfill in Christ.

1 Corinthians 4:15: "*For though ye have ten thousand instructors in*

Christ, yet ye have not many fathers; for in Christ Jesus I have begotten you through the Gospel" (KJV, 1998).

Chapter 2

Absence of a Father's Love

There have been many accounts of children their parents have abandoned at birth, and because of this, these children are left with emotional scars that haunt them most of their lives.

In my early years of counseling, I had the opportunity to work with emotionally disturbed youth ranging in ages from 13 to 19. The stories they shared with me detailing their feelings of isolation and instability because of shuffling between foster homes were heartbreaking and tragic. They shared accounts of verbal and physical abuse—even to the extent of rape. Some of the children even spoke of times when they were left locked away in dark places for extended periods.

I was consistently asked by some of the youth, *"Why do you think my parents abandoned me? Do you think they ever think about me?"* They would often wonder if anything was wrong with them; their inner pain was evident. At times, as most counselors do, I felt inadequately equipped to assist them in resolving the deep-seated issues they developed because of abandonment.

Attempting to walk through the feelings of rejection and abandonment can leave youth with the emotional trauma that takes a lifetime to recover. The number of children who are abandoned in America each year is staggering. Seven thousand children are left each year. (Encyclopedia of Children's Health, n.d.) Forty thousand new infants are placed in foster care each year (ABC News, 2006). Unfortunately, the trauma they experience often results in unhealthy patterns of behavior. Some of these patterns of behavior are:

- always wanting to please others (being a "people pleaser")
- giving too much in relationships
- an inability to trust others
- pushing others away to avoid rejection
- feeling insecure in romantic partnerships and friendships
- Codependency
- a need for continual reassurance that others love them and will stay with them
- the need to control others
- persisting with unhealthy relationships
- the inability to maintain relationships
- moving quickly from one relationship to another
- sabotaging relationships
- lack of emotional intimacy
- constant worry about being abandoned
- separation anxiety
- clinginess
- fear of being alone, including at bedtime

- frequent illness which often has no apparent physical cause
- isolation
- low self-esteem

In severe cases, such as those in which a child has experienced the loss of a parent or caregiver, children may develop unhealthy ways of coping, such as addiction, disordered eating, aggression toward others, and/or self-harm (Leonard, 2020).

For some, the inability to cope with the underlying issues that result from abandonment leads to a life of crime. In contrast, others develop behaviors that can be categorized as mental disorders. Two of these such disorders are Borderline Personality Disorder and Separation Anxiety Disorder.

Borderline Personality Disorder is defined as a pervasive pattern of instability of interpersonal relationships, self-image, and affects, and is marked by impulsivity, beginning by early adulthood and present in a variety of contexts, as indicated by five of the following from this abbreviated list:

1. Frantic efforts to avoid real or imagined abandonment.
2. A pattern of unstable and intense interpersonal relationships characterized by alternating between extremes of idealization and devaluation.
3. Identity disturbance: markedly and persistently unstable self-image or sense of self.

4. Impulsivity in at least two of the following areas that are potentially self-damaging: spending, sex, substance abuse, reckless driving, binge eating.
5. Recurrent suicidal behavior, gestures, or threats, or self-mutilating behavior.
6. Affective instability due to marked reactivity of mood (e.g., intense episodic dysphoria, irritability, or anxiety usually lasting a few hours and only rarely more than a few days).
7. Chronic feelings of emptiness.

Children left unprotected by parents are more vulnerable to sexual predators who engage in inappropriate behavior toward minors. The following statistics attest to this:

- 1 in 4 girls and 1 in 6 boys will be sexually abused before they turn 18.
- Over 65,000 children were sexually abused in 2016.
- 8.6 % of reported child abuse cases were sexual abuse.
- 34% of people who sexually abuse a child are family members.
- 12.3% of girls were age ten or younger at the time of their first rape/victimization, and 30% of girls were between 11 and 17.
- 27.8% of boys were age ten or younger at the time of their first rape/victimization.

- 96% of people who sexually abuse children are male, and 76.8% of people who sexually abuse children are adults.
- 325,000 children are at risk of becoming victims of commercial child sexual exploitation each year.
- The average age at which girls first become victims of prostitution is 12 to 14 years old, and the average age for boys is 11 to 13 years old (American SPCC, 2021).

Neglect remains the number one form of abuse. More children die from neglect than any other form of child abuse. One area often overlooked when we examine the child's well-being is the biological parent's divorce. Often, separation and divorce are minimized as a way of life and something that the child must accept. It does not consider the detrimental impact that this break in their usual way of life has on the child psychologically and emotionally.

But divorce is more than an issue of social capital or simple psychology (like self-esteem), for we are more than our place in the structures of society. Even if young people preserve their social capital and understand why their parents split up and what divorce means, it still leaves a mark that cannot be erased by retained social capital or correct knowledge. And these marks last well beyond the age of custody because divorce is ontological.

Ontological security is a sense of safety; it is confidence and trust that the natural and social worlds are as they appear to be. Giddens explains the phrase *"ontological security"* as the confidence that most human beings have in the continuity of their self-identity and in the constancy of the surrounding social and material environments of action" (Root, 2010).

In his book, The Children of Divorce, Andrew Root explained that whenever a child's parents go through a divorce, it leaves the child with a loss of identity and a sense of incompleteness—a sense of being a half and no longer a whole of both parents. It affects the child emotionally, spiritually, physically, socially, and mentally. It further damages the child when the departing parent no longer interacts with the child.

When we examine the life of Joseph, we can see the immediate effects of forced separation from a parent. In this biblical account, we first see a son who experiences the love and affection of his father to such a degree that it provokes his brothers to hate and jealousy. Jacob, the father of Joseph, showered him with preferential attention and care. One day Joseph's father presented him with a gift of endearment, a coat of many colors. This gesture intensified the hate that Joseph's brothers had toward him (Genesis 37:3-4).

As you read the history of this family, it is easy to identify where the problem began. While running away to hide from his brother Esau, Jacob ends up near his future father-in-law, Laban, who lived with his family. The Bible says Jacob came upon a well where one of Laban's daughters, Rachel, watered her father's flock. When Jacob saw her, he immediately fell in love with her; not long after that, Jacob asked Laban to marry Rachel. Laban consented but imposed a stipulation that required Jacob to work seven years for her hand in marriage. Jacob acquiesced in laboring for the seven years, but Laban deceived him. After working seven years for Rachel's hand in marriage, Jacob awoke from a drunken stupor the morning after his wedding to discover that Leah, Laban's oldest daughter, not Rachel, was in his matrimonial bed.

Can you imagine the horror and disappointment Jacob must have experienced? Laban was a man of tradition. When Jacob approached Laban to inquire why he had deceived him in such a manner, Laban said it was never the custom for the younger daughter to marry before the eldest daughter. So, Jacob had to work an additional seven years for the hand of Rachel, whom he truly loved. After a total of fourteen years of labor, Jacob and Rachel finally wed.

However, more challenges arose when it came to Rachel bearing children. While Leah, the wife Jacob, married through deception, was having children, Rachel was in misery because, for a time, she was childless. The difficulty in childbearing coupled with Jacob's genuine love for her caused Jacob to become attached to Rachel's children. The love that Jacob had for Rachel was now transferred to his first child with Rachel, Joseph. Jacob preferred Joseph more than all the sons that Leah and her handmaids had borne for him. This love/loveless house of relationships became the breeding ground for hate, division, and jealousy.

As evidence of this preferential treatment, Jacob does something for Joseph that distinguishes Joseph from his brothers. Jacob presents Joseph with a coat of many colors. This coat represented many things, but I will pinpoint only a few.

Foremost, it represented Jacob's deep love and affection for his son Joseph. It was not that he did not love his other sons, but Joseph revealed the depth of Jacob's love for Joseph's mother, Rachel. Joseph was a product of the strength of Jacob's old age. Secondly, the coat of many colors was given as a covering, but it was more than a natural covering; it was a covering of blessings, protection, and covenant. Even when Joseph was not in possession of the coat, the coat would continue to be a potent symbol of protection for Joseph while remaining a symbol of vengeance and retribution for his brothers.

One day Joseph's father sent him out to find his brothers as they fed the flock at Shechem. Joseph eventually joined up with them at Dothan. Joseph's brothers came up with a scheme to take the coat of many colors, put animal's blood on it and tell their father, Jacob, that a wild animal had killed Joseph. Therefore, when the coat was brought back to their father without Joseph, it got Jacob's heart into a deep state of grief (Genesis 37:17-35).

This coat of many colors covered in blood painted a picture of how Jacob could not provide the covering that Joseph needed at the most critical time of his life, despite his intention to. In contrast, stripping Joseph of his coat of many colors meant the end of the preferential treatment for Joseph's brothers. Could it be that now that the coat of many colors was no longer in Joseph's possession that Joseph would now be left without the evidence of his father's love, care, and protection? The love/loveless relationship between Jacob, Leah, and Rachel spread like cancer to the next generation.

While they abandoned their brother and left him for dead, a divine setup occurred because Joseph ended up in chains as a slave in Potiphar's house. Potiphar was an officer of Pharaoh, a captain of the guard (Genesis 37:36). Joseph found himself separated from his father's love and care, from everything he knew to be familiar, and from the comfort of being home. At 17-years-old, his life was turned upside down.

Although he may have been outside the reach of his earthly father, he was still within reach of his Heavenly Father. Many children are left alone and abandoned, unable to fight or defend themselves, and because of this, they eventually find themselves in precarious and harmful situations. These children sometimes find their way into the communities of our church. And though their earthly fathers have abandoned them, we can offer them the spiritual guidance and love they need to help them find the right direction as pastors and church leaders.

While serving as interim pastor at a particular church, I met a young man who had found his way to the church. He was an intelligent and polite young man who appeared to be in search of something. As we developed a bond, he detailed his upbringing. He shared overcoming issues of homelessness and not having food and proper clothing to wear. His mother tried her best to provide for him and his siblings. Though she tried to do all that she could do, she fell short. His time spent at the church and the relationship we developed was instrumental in helping him find his bearings. Today, he is a college graduate with a very successful and lucrative career who wants to give back as I have given him.

Imagine how many young people's lives can be changed for the better if there were just more spiritual fathers who took the time to listen and impart some wisdom to them. We cannot neglect how God strategically places "destiny helpers" in our path and how at other times, we become destiny helpers in another's path.

As we continue to look at the life of Joseph, we can see where God put people of means and influence in his life who helped him get from one plateau to the next. Though Joseph was no longer in possession of the coat of many colors, we see how he still possessed everything that coat represented—the love of his father, divine covering, and covenant blessings.

Genesis 39:2-4: "*And the Lord was with Joseph, and he was a prosperous man; and he was in the house of his master the Egyptian. And his master saw that the Lord was with him, and that the Lord made all that he did to prosper in his hand. And Joseph found grace in his sight, and he served him: and he made him overseer over his house, and all that he had he put into his hand.*"

Much like how Joseph found himself in a strange land, children who go off to universities often find themselves in unfamiliar environments and are among people with diverse beliefs that conflict with what they have been taught. In these new communities, youths sometimes feel ill-equipped to deal with the challenges they face. Again, this is where spiritual fathers can serve as safe havens *if* they are intentional about making the connection.

As I reflect on my college years, I, like most incoming college students, experienced culture shock. All of my education before college was predominantly afro-centric, but now the predominant culture would be euro-centric. I was taught to perceive Christianity from a very conservative view but now found people of like faith who approached many issues from a more liberal perspective than what I had become accustomed to. This new environment that I called home most of the year was more like a melting pot of people from all over the world, unlike where I was raised.

It was at this time that God provided three central figures in my life. Two of them were Bishop Wallace and Lady Dorothy Sibley. The Sibleys were caring and loving. They extended themselves not only to me but to a group of others and embraced us as their own family. The Sibleys became the parents we needed while we were away from home. They often opened their home to us on weekends, feeding us and imparting spiritual truth and wisdom. I distinctly remember Bishop Sibley asking the question, *"How do you learn how to preach?"* His answer was profound yet simple. *"You learn how to preach by preaching."* Bishop Sibley's words echoed the adage which says practice makes perfect. He not only spoke these words into my life, but he followed up by providing opportunities for many young ministers like myself to teach and preach the Word of God.

Another person who served as a destiny helper in my life is Bishop Claudius C. Pratt. Bishop Pratt invested in my life while I was in college. I can recall being in a car accident one night coming from a part-time job I had. The car that my father had purchased for me was totaled. My father contacted Bishop Pratt, who was in Cleveland, Tennessee, serving as the Director of Black Ministries for the Church of God. Bishop Pratt patiently walked me through the process of dealing with the insurance company and advised me on the process of going to the dealership to purchase a new car.

In these instances and others, while living in an unfamiliar place, God provided spiritual parents who made my experience easier and more pleasant to navigate. Joseph went through something similar. Although he was in a place of unfamiliarity, God gave him favor with the people who influenced him to make his experience more bearable and easier to navigate.

Joseph's climb to authority came with many highs and lows. At one point, he finds himself in trouble after refusing Potiphar's wife's sexual advances. Enraged by his refusal to submit to her desires, Potiphar's wife falsely accuses Joseph of rape. Potiphar immediately had Joseph was thrown into prison (Genesis 39:7-20).

Again, Joseph faced a low. First, his brothers took his coat of many colors, now Potiphar's wife attempted to taint his character. The butler would eventually forget Joseph, and he helped deliver him out of prison by his gift of interpreting dreams (Genesis 40:23).

God arranged it so that Pharaoh would dream a dream that no one would be able to interpret. When the butler hears of the Pharaoh's inability to interpret his dream, he remembers Joseph, who he left behind in prison. Through Joseph's life, you hear the words abandoned, left behind, forsaken; but when God has purposed something for your life, there is nothing that will prevent His will from coming to pass.

Joseph's ability to interpret Pharoah's dream was key to Egypt's survival, and as a result, Pharoah appointed Joseph as second in command in Egypt (Genesis 41:41). Joseph was not just the key to Egypt's survival, but as destiny would have it, he preserved his own family, of which his father Jacob was the patriarch. It would be through Jacob that a nation would be birthed. God's divine providence was evident in the life of Joseph.

Isaiah 46:10: *"Declaring the end from the beginning, and from ancient times the things that are not yet done, saying, My counsel shall stand, and I will do all my pleasure"* (KJV, 1998).

Ecclesiastes 3:14: *"I know that, whatsoever God doeth, it shall be for ever: nothing can be put to it, nor any thing taken from it: and God doeth it, that men should fear before him"* (KJV, 1998).

With all the pitfalls and setbacks that Joseph experienced, he could have set off on a path of destructive behavior. Statistical data supports the fact that youth with abandonment trauma tend to internalize the pain and exhibit detrimental behavior to their future and others around them. But Joseph's outcomes did not match this statistic. Joseph would be reunited with the brothers that betrayed him. Because of Joseph's interpretation of Pharaoh's dream, Egypt became the breadbasket for neighboring countries. We see Joseph exercise restraint even when he could have exercised vengeance once he reunited with his brothers when they came to Egypt seeking food during the famine (Genesis 42:7).

The brothers immediately thought within themselves that Joseph would take vengeance on them for the cruelty they had shown to him in the past. But Joseph responded, *"God sent me before you to preserve you a posterity in the earth and to save your lives by a great deliverance. So now it was not you that sent me hither, but God: and he hath made me a father to Pharaoh, and lord of all his house, and a ruler throughout all the land of Egypt"* (Genesis 45:7-8).

Joseph would also be eventually reunited with his father. The abandoned son had now become the salvation of Israel. There was a moment of exhilaration and relief as Joseph prepared his chariot and went out to meet his father as he approached Goshen. When Joseph reaches his father, he is filled with emotion. He fell on his father's neck and remained there for a space of time. Thirteen years had passed since Jacob had beheld the eyes of his son, Joseph. Those were thirteen *long* years of separation and living with the false realization that his beloved son was deceased.

Joseph might have been justified to have a seed of bitterness in his heart toward his brothers. Imagine the thirteen birthdays that were missed with his father and others. Jacob did not have the honor of celebrating the marriage of Joseph to his wife, Asenath, daughter of Potipherah, priest of On (Genesis 41:45). Joseph did not get to share the joy of the birth of his sons Manasseh and Ephraim with his father, Jacob. But even in that, there is great healing in his sons' names. Manasseh means "the Lord hath made me forget my pain." The name Ephraim means "the Lord has made me fruitful in the days of my captivity." God blessed Joseph despite his pain. His sons would be constant reminders that even in his time of abandonment, God had not forgotten about him. The reunion of Joseph with his father was a bittersweet moment, one of joy and celebration and one of loss and disappointment.

I believe all the pain and hurt Joseph had to endure had been swallowed up in the joy that he experienced the moment he was able to feel the embrace of his father's arms again. On the other hand, Jacob finally felt at peace to transition from this life. His son, that was lost, was now found. This is the joy that every son and daughter should experience when connected to spiritual fathers and mothers who will help them heal from the pain of being abandoned and forgotten.

This is the cry that I have heard from many young ministers in the past. Many ministers leave the ministry wounded, broken, and disillusioned because they felt thrown to wolves, left to fight for themselves without an umbrella of support and protection. Like

Joseph, they felt abandoned by their brothers and sisters in ministry. As a result, they became casualties of the spiritual warfare that leaves silenced churches in their tracks. Robert Russell said that one of the primary reasons ministers drop out of the ministry is inexplicable loneliness (Russell, 2019).

Seventy percent of pastors do not have a close pastor friend. For most pastors, loneliness is a horrible certainty.

The stark reality of pastoring is that the workload extends beyond 70 hours weekly—a pastor's work is never done. Cultivating relationships with parishioners is another challenge. Pastors have to work with them daily and weekly, often counseling them on many different issues, attempting to mend or encourage others in their marriage, career, finances, health, and spiritual challenges. Most of the calls a pastor receives are dealing with parishioner complaints while at the same time having to navigate personal distresses alone.

"Most ministers feel they cannot share their feelings with other ministers - too many churches are in competition with one another, this may be the ammunition they need! And when ministers attend denominational meetings, so often others around them only give "praise reports" that lend themselves to believing something is wrong with a minister who has problems" (Fuller, 2020).

Steve Statz provides some vital statistics on the welfare of ministers:

- 80% believe pastoral ministry has negatively affected their families. Many pastor's children do not attend church because of what the church has done to their parents

- 33% state that being in the ministry is an outright hazard to their family
- 75% report significant stress-related crisis at least once in their ministry
- 90% feel they are inadequately trained to cope with the ministry demands
- 50% feel unable to meet the demands of the job of a pastor
- 70% say they have a lower self-image now than when they first started
- 70% do not have someone they consider a close friend
- 40% report serious conflict with a parishioner at least once a month
- 33% confess having been involved in inappropriate sexual behavior with someone in the church
- 50% have considered leaving the ministry in the last few months
- 50% of the ministers starting will not last 5 years
- Only 1 out of every 10 ministers will actually retire as a minister in some form
- 94% of clergy families feel the pressures of the pastor's ministry

Just as Joseph experienced abandonment by his brothers, we have pastors frustrated and depressed due to also feeling abandoned. There is the need for restoration and healing in the Body of Christ on all fronts. The reconnection of Joseph and Jacob sets a model for establishing biblical structures that will provide care and strength to pastors and spiritual sons and daughters who find themselves alone and abandoned.

Today's sons and daughters need to feel that there is a covenant group of ministers bonded together to provide counsel and support to them in their times of struggle. These avenues of strength are critical because they provide places of healing and renewal much needed in the Body of Christ. Unhealthy leaders can't lead healthy congregations. But when spiritual sons and daughters who have experienced abandonment can receive the warmth and care of spiritual leaders, it will reassure them that they are not alone and provide avenues for healing and restoration.

Chapter 3

Absence of a Father's Voice

One Saturday evening, when I was about six years old, I had fallen asleep, and my parents thought I would remain asleep for the rest of the night. They thought they could make a quick run to my grandmother's house and return before I woke up. Startled by the thought, I instinctively began to set out walking toward my grandmother's house. As life would have it, I awoke to an empty house. I can distinctly remember hearing the music from the series Hawaii Five-0 playing in the background. When I called out for my father and got no response, I realized that I was home alone.

The neighborhood I grew up in was known for distributing drugs, violence, and undercover prostitution, but even amid all that, there were some fine people spread within that community. My father served as deacon and church clerk at that time. He would take many neighborhood children to church in what we jokingly called the roach mobile—not because the car had roaches, but because it was a very old car. My father became a father figure to many of the children in the neighborhood because many of the neighborhood youths had absentee fathers.

Now having painted a picture of this environment, can you imagine the panic I experienced when I awoke to the absence of my father's voice in the house? Our house was dark, and the only thing I could hear was the television.

In search of the comfort of my father's voice, I ventured out to my grandmother's house. This was not an easy task, especially for a little boy of no more than six years old. It was dangerous enough to attempt the journey during daylight, but it was an entirely different issue to travel this distance during the night. There was an open field that I had to cross and walkthrough, which led to 62nd street. 62nd street was an incredibly high traffic area known for bars, pool halls, gambling, and heavily populated by people looking to engage in criminal activity. Through the peril, I would eventually find myself at the doorstep of my grandmother's house.

I left a safe place in search of a safe place but somehow found myself walking through many unsafe situations. That is how important my father's voice was to me. When his voice was absent in my life just for a moment, fear and anxiety gripped my young mind and spirit. My father's voice was a sound of security, assuring me that no matter what could go wrong, everything would be alright. His voice was a sound of strength and courage. Because of his voice in the house, I felt I could rest in the serenity of the night hours.

Too often, children in similar circumstances find themselves journeying from safe places because of the absence of a father's voice. They find themselves in dangerous environments that are detrimental to their safety and well-being.

It is vital for people looking to venture out and set their mark on society to have spiritual fathers who will speak words of affirmation and security into their lives. Spiritual fathers possess a voice of strength and courage that helps guide and protect their spiritual children from the pitfalls and dangers that lie ahead of them. Throughout my life, I saw how God used the voice of spiritual fathers to keep me from dangers seen and unseen.

The influence of a father's voice in the house commands respect and discipline. There is something about the base inflection of the man's voice that commands obedience. I remember how my sisters and I would respond when my father was at home. We did not listen to our mother, but there was just a different level of respect that our father's voice commanded. His voice said there is power and strength in the house that motherly nurturing cannot duplicate.

I often put it this way, and *dads love their children more dangerously*. I mean that they express their love and bond through roughhousing and are more likely to encourage risk-taking. They provide kids with a broader diversity of social experiences; they also introduce them to various methods of dealing with life. Fathers tend to stress rules, justice, fairness, and duty in the discipline. In this way, they teach children the objectivity and consequences of right and wrong. They give kids insight into the world of men. They prepare them for life's challenges and demonstrate by example the meaning of respect between the sexes. In connection with this last point, research indicates that a married father is substantially less likely to abuse his wife or children than men in any other category (Popenoe, 2011).

Fathers encourage competition, engendering independence.

Mothers promote equity, creating a sense of security. Dads emphasize conceptual communication, which helps kids expand their vocabulary and intellectual capacities—Moms major in sympathy, care, and support, thus demonstrating the importance of relationships. Dads tend to see their children in relation to the rest of the world. Mothers tend to see the rest of the world regarding their children. Neither style of parenting is adequate by itself. Taken together, they balance each other out and equip the up-and-coming generation with a healthy, well-rounded approach to life (Popenoe, 2011).

Most research indicates that babies can recognize their father's voice from 32 weeks gestation and immediately after birth (Grace Y. Lee, 2014). As far as facial recognition goes, that takes a bit more time. It is also said that a father can bond with his newborn within six months if time is spent interacting with the infant (Williams, 2020). Fathers have always been seen as more like a spare part than an essential part of the child's development.

When my daughter Ashley was just days old, I would take her in my arms and rock her to sleep. I often did that, and my wife felt at ease with my ability to comfort our daughter while she rested from a long day of caring for a newborn. What made putting my daughter to sleep easier was the fact that she became familiar with my voice. It was not that my voice was soothing or melodic, but the fact that it was a familiar voice; that represented protection and care to her.

What does it mean to have the voice of a father or a father

figure speaking into the life of a child? For Jesus, the Son of God, the Savior of the world, it meant everything.

Mark 15:34: *"And at the ninth hour, Jesus cried with a loud voice, saying, Eloi, Eloi, Lama Sabacthani? Which is translated, My God, My God, why have you forsaken me?"*

The paradox of this scripture is that of an obedient son abandoned by a distant father when the father was never absent from the presence of his son. It appears to be one of the darkest moments in Jesus's earthly life. Jesus had just undergone the most excruciating experience, even to the point of enduring the cross and despising the shame.

Jesus was humiliated, stripped of his garments, and spat upon. They smote Him, jeered Him, plucked His beard, and they stuck a crown of thorns on His brows. The Roman crown of thorns had 72 thorns in it. The Roman soldiers forced Him to carry His method of execution up Golgotha's hill. They placed a sign above Him mocking His identity— *Hail, the King of the Jews.* They put spikes in His hands and His feet. Jesus endured *all* this after having taken thirty-nine stripes on His back. The soldiers used a weapon known as cat-of-nine tails: it had leather straps rippled with particles of glass, metal, broken bones, and thorns. They used this to rip the flesh from His bones with every strike (Matthew 27:33-46).

My God, My God, why hast thou forsaken me—but in that hour of torture and suffering, there was no response from His Heavenly

Father. There was silence as He was suspended between heaven and earth; silence when all the weight of the world rested upon His shoulders.

Isaiah 53:4-5: *"Surely, he has borne our griefs, and carried our sorrows: Yet he esteemed him stricken, smitten by God and afflicted, but he was wounded for our transgressions, He was bruised for our iniquities. The chastisement of our peace was upon Him, and by His stripes we are healed"* (Version, 1998).

Jesus had beheld the bitter cup of sin, death, and the grave as He entered the Garden of Gethsemane to pray, *"Father, if it be possible, let this cup pass from me"* (Matthew 26:39). He prayed this prayer three times, but He went one step further; He submitted His will to the Father's will, saying, *"nevertheless not my will but thine will be done."* He humbled Himself even unto death, the death of the cross.

With the world's future at stake, Christ died for all of humanity. With all of this in view, what happened to His Father's voice? The voice He craved to hear in this moment of purpose. At other moments in Jesus' life, Jesus listened to the Father's voice of affirmation and affection. At Jesus' baptism at the Jordan, John the Baptist wrestled with the thought of baptizing Christ. When John the Baptist saw Jesus walking toward him, he said, *"Behold! The Lamb of God, which taketh away the sins of the world"* (John 1:29). The Bible records that at Jesus' baptism, the heavens were opened to Him. The Spirit of God rested upon Him like a dove, and the Father spoke. *"This is my beloved Son, in whom I am well pleased"* (Mark 1:11).

The Father declared pleasure in the work and purpose of His Son. It provides added encouragement to a son when he knows he has the approval and support of his father.

I could see my father's face as it would light up when he would see me preaching at an event or orating at a school function. When I graduated from college, my father told me, *"You can go even further,"* and it was those words that helped propel me to heights that I never thought I could achieve. Sadly, that type of affirmation is absent in so many sons and daughters' lives—the voice of wise counsel, the voice of support and encouragement. Jesus had this affirmation from His Heavenly Father.

There was another occasion at the Mount of Transfiguration when Jesus had taken Peter, James, and John up into a mountain to pray. It was there that Moses and Elijah appeared before them in conversation with Jesus. When the disciples saw this phenomenon, they said to each other, *"Let us build three tabernacles, one for Elijah, one for Moses and another for Jesus."* But God spoke resounding words of affection concerning *His* Son, Jesus— *"This is my beloved son in whom I am well pleased, Hear ye him"* (Matthew 17:5).

The Father not only shared His affection for His Son, but He distinguished His relationship with His Son from His relationship with Moses and Elijah. Moses had led Israel out of Egypt, across the Red Sea, just outside the Promised Land, yet he could not be spoken of in the same breath as Jesus.

Elijah saw the fire come down from Heaven and prayed until rain fell after a three-year drought had plagued the land. Elijah performed miracles, even the miracle of raising a dead boy back to life, but his feats dulled compared to the power and might of Jesus. There was no comparison to be drawn. God Himself made an emphatic statement of His Son's mission and purpose.

We have these occasions that have been recorded of the Father vocally hovering over His Son. Yet while Jesus hung on the cross between two thieves, the voice of the Father was absent. What appears to be a contradiction of support and care is, in reality, the action of a loving Father. *How?* God the Father and God the Son had agreed about fulfilling the assignment that had to be carried out.

> Luke 24:25-27: *"Then he said unto them, O fools, and slow of heart to believe all that the prophets have spoken: Ought not Christ to have suffered these things, and to enter into his glory? And beginning at Moses and all the prophets, he expounded unto them in all the scriptures the things concerning himself"* (KJV, 1998).

> Hebrews 10:5-7: *"Wherefore when he cometh into the world, he saith, Sacrifice and offering thou wouldest not, but a body hast thou prepared me: In burnt offerings and sacrifices for sin thou hast had no pleasure. Then said I, Lo, I come (in the volume of the book it is written of me,) to do thy will, O God"* (KJV, 1998).

> Genesis 3:15: *"And I will put enmity between thee and the woman, and between thy seed and her seed; it shall bruise thy head, and thou*

> *shalt bruise his heel"* (KJV, 1998).
>
> Revelation 13:8: *"And all that dwell upon the earth shall worship him, whose names are not written in the book of life of the Lamb slain from the foundation of the world"* (KJV, 1998).
>
> Luke 22:42: *"Saying, Father, if thou be willing, remove this cup from me: nevertheless, not my will, but thine, be done"* (Version, 1998).

These scriptures reveal that although the Father's voice in that particular moment was silent, Jesus had foreknown and accepted that His suffering and eventual death would be for a divine purpose. Although Jesus did not hear the voice of the Father responding to His cry, He knew that His Father was in total control of what was taking place. This is why when Jesus gave up the ghost, He could say, *"It is finished"* and *"Into thine hands I commend my Spirit"* because the assignment was completed (John 19:30).

> Philippians 2:8-11: *"And being found in fashion as a man, he humbled himself, and became obedient unto death, even the death of the cross. Wherefore God also hath highly exalted him and given him a name which is above every name: That at the name of Jesus every knee should bow, of things in heaven, and things in earth, and things under the earth; that every tongue should confess that Jesus Christ is Lord, to the glory of God the Father."*

Just as Jesus sought the affirmation of His Father, children need direction and leadership from a father or father-like figure. They need a voice of authority speaking into their ears as they deal with difficult situations and make decisions during times of conflict. The voice of a father is guiding; it is the voice that declares, *"This is how to act in this situation,* or *No, that's not how we roll."*

Through my own experiences, I have learned the importance of that father's voice in a child's life, even if that child is an adult.

My father passed away on December 12, 1997. I did not fully comprehend the depth of the impact of his death until months afterward. For a few months, I felt like my life was out of balance. My father's voice was now absent in times of significant decision-making and during critical transition points in my life. The things which gave me the resolve to move forward at these times were echoes of my father's voice of wisdom and the comfort and reassurance from my God, my Heavenly Father.

While interning at the Community Retreat Center in Hartford, Connecticut, I had the opportunity to counsel young men. Many of them gravitated toward me because I could provide the wisdom and direction that had been absent for most of their journeys until that point. The supervisor allowed me to run group sessions with men grappling with brokenness, lack of purpose, and a diminished sense of self-worth or identity. Unfortunately, this is the state that many young people are currently in, many of them waiting on some positive role models to speak into their lives and inspire change in the trajectory of their courses.

2 Samuel 7:14-15: *"I will be his father, and he shall be my son. If he*

> *commits iniquity, I will chasten him with the rod of men, and with the stripes of the children of men: But my mercy shall not depart away from him, as I took it from Saul, whom I put away before thee."*

These powerful words of love and fidelity God speak to David as He shares with him that He will establish a kingdom through a son from his seed. God affirmed that He would never take back His love from his son even if David's son failed him. This is a message of commitment that establishes a model of compassion, affirmation, love, and unconditional support for fathers toward their children—a voice in a child's life-affirming love and support no matter what comes.

Too often, a father's love and support come with a price or with conditions. But God's love toward us is unconditional, perpetual, and endures throughout generations.

Spiritual fathers who care for sons and daughters by speaking spiritual vitality into their children's lives have the incredible potential to affect the world at large.

Consider this information given to us by Dr. Edward Kruk, in *Psychology Today: Father Absence, Father Deficit, Father Hinge, The Vital Importance of Paternal Presence in Children's Lives.* When fathers are disengaged from their children's lives, researchers have found that for children, the results are nothing short of disastrous, along with several dimensions:

- Diminished self-concept and compromised physical and emotional security: Children consistently report feeling abandoned when their fathers are not involved in their lives, struggling with their emotions, and episodic bouts of self-loathing.
- Behavioral problems: Fatherless children have more difficulties with social adjustment and are more likely to report problems with friendships and manifest behavior problems; many develop a swaggering, intimidating persona to disguise their underlying fears, resentments, anxieties, and unhappiness.
- Truancy and poor academic performance: 71 percent of high school dropouts are fatherless; fatherless children have more trouble academically, scoring poorly on tests of reading, mathematics, and thinking skills; children from father-absent homes are more likely to play truant from school, more likely to be excluded from school, more likely to leave school at age 16, and less likely to attain academic and professional qualifications in adulthood.
- Delinquency and youth crime, including violent crime: 85 percent of youth in prison have an absent father; fatherless children are more likely to offend and go to jail as adults.
- Promiscuity and teen pregnancy: Fatherless children are more likely to experience problems with sexual

health, including a greater likelihood of having intercourse before the age of 16, foregoing contraception during first intercourse, becoming teenage parents, and contracting sexually transmitted infection; many girls manifest an object hunger for males, and in experiencing the emotional loss of their fathers egocentrically as a rejection of them, may become susceptible to exploitation by adult men.

- Drug and alcohol abuse: Fatherless children are more likely to smoke, drink alcohol, and abuse drugs in childhood and adulthood.
- Homelessness: 90 percent of runaway children have an absent father.
- Exploitation and abuse: Fatherless children are at greater risk of suffering physical, emotional, and sexual abuse, being five times more likely to have experienced physical abuse and emotional maltreatment, with a one hundred times higher risk of fatal abuse; a recent study reported that preschoolers not living with both of their biological parents are 40 times more likely to be sexually abused.
- Physical health problems: Fatherless children report significantly more psychosomatic health symptoms and illnesses such as acute and chronic pain, asthma, headaches, and stomach aches.

- Mental health disorders: Father-absent children are consistently overrepresented in many mental health problems, particularly anxiety, depression, and suicide.
- Life chances: As adults, fatherless children are more likely to experience unemployment, have low incomes, remain on social assistance, and experience homelessness.
- Future relationships: Father-absent children tend to enter partnerships earlier, are more likely to divorce or dissolve their cohabiting unions and are more likely to have children outside marriage or any partnership.
- Mortality: Fatherless children are more likely to die as children and live an average of four years less over their life span (Edward Kruk, 2012).

Given that these and other social problems correlate more strongly with fatherlessness than with any other factor—surpassing race, social class, and poverty—paternal absence may well be the most critical social issue of our time. In *Fatherless America*, David Blankenhorn calls the crisis of fatherless children *"the most destructive trend of our generation"* (Blankenhorn, 1995). A recent British report from the University of Birmingham, *"Dad and Me,"* confirms Blankenhorn's claims, concluding that the need for a father is on an epidemic scale, and "father deficit" should be treated as a public health issue (Edward Kruk, 2012).

As God, the Father spoke words of affirmation and assurance

into the life of His Son Jesus, so our children should be fortunate enough to hear the voice of positive affirmation in their ears.

That night when I awoke to my father's absence troubled me to my core—imagine this is the daily reality of many young men and women. With this thought in mind, I am compelled to challenge spiritual fathers to be that voice that fills this paternal vacuum.

"A value of a father has no price." (Natalie Book)

"A dad is the anchor upon which his children stand. (Anonymous)

"When a father speaks, may his children hear the love in his voice above all else." (Willie M. Munday)

Chapter 4

Absence of a Father's Touch

Many a day, I can recall walking to the neighborhood store for my grandmother, Georgiana Ramsey, and her neighbor who lived across the street, Laura Evans. Both women were assertive. At that time, it seemed like an arduous chore, but in retrospect, it taught me respect and discipline. The years I spent living with my grandmother instilled in me a great sense of appreciation for the elderly and the wisdom they possess. It was like learning about life without having to experience some of its harsh realities. I was being mentored without even realizing it.

Fast forward to years later, when I was tasked with the occasional responsibility of chauffeuring the State Bishops to their council meeting in Cocoa Beach, Florida, most young ministers would have seen it as a bothersome task. Their meetings often lasted the entire day, and the drive was up to six hours roundtrip, but I viewed it as a unique learning experience. I had unrestricted access to hear them talk about the struggles and challenges they faced in pastoring—and hear each offer the other different solutions. It was like being in seminary without the desks, lectures, and textbooks. These were real-time practical lessons. The lessons I learned in that setting have been invaluable in the course of my ministry.

Bishop Elkanah Hepburn played a particularly pivotal role in my life. I endearingly like to remember him as Bishop Encourager; he was like a silent spiritual father. He spoke into my life on occasions when I felt like my ministry had hit a crossroad. He probably said less than a thousand words directly to me in the time that I knew him. It was not what he said but what he did that made the difference.

Too often, leaders are placed in positions of power and authority, and rather than reach back and pull others up with them; they utilize their position to hold others down. This was not the case with Bishop Encourager.

I remember when my supervising pastor told me that I was too young to move up in rank in the ministry, though others my age had been promoted. Bishop Encourager took the opportunity to commit to helping me. When the promotion test was released, he looked to ensure I completed the application and was set forth in ministry. Bishop Encourager did the same thing for many other ministers. Today, I realize that the doors God has privileged me to walk through were made accessible by the spiritual fathers God placed in my life, like Bishop Encourager and Bishop Preaching Machine.

Bishop Preaching Machine, whose real name was Bishop Sellers, was celebrated for his gift of relaying the stories of the Bible in such a unique way. One of his messages was "*One More Night with the Frogs.*"

From the time I was 14 years old, I recall seeing this man travel from city to city preaching to packed-out crowds. Bishop

Sellers' messages had catchy titles and powerful illustrations. He achieved many great things throughout his ministry. Because of him, I had the opportunity to speak on one of the greatest platforms of my life, and since that time, many other doors have opened. One door became the beginning of a domino effect that has carried me around the world. I appreciate these two men and the others who have touched my life in such an undeniable way.

A *Psychology Today* article entitled, *"What Happens if You Don't Touch Your Baby"* explores the importance of physical touch to the vitality of an infant (Szalavitz, 2010).

"Babies who are not held, nuzzled, and hugged enough can stop growing, and if the situation lasts long enough, even die. Researchers discovered this when trying to figure out why some orphanages had infant mortality rates around 30-40%" (Szalavitz, 2010).

Scientific America reports, *"Many children who have not had ample physical and emotional attention are at higher risk for behavioral, emotional and social problems as they grow up. These trends point to the lasting effects of early infancy environments and the changes that the brain undergoes during that period"* (Harmon, 2010).

I believe there is a parallel between the importance of touch for infants and the importance of contact in the lives of spiritual sons and daughters. There have been times in my ministry where words have failed, but I was able to find solace and comfort in the reassuring embrace of my father.

There is a vacuum in our world for spiritual parents. We need spiritual fathers and mothers who take the opportunity to be physically present to pour into the lives of young ministers.

Elisha was that presence in the life of young King Joash. Despite failing to heed Elisha's wise counsel for much of his reign, Joash did feel the impact of Elisha's spiritual presence in the nation.

The Bible says of King Joash that he did evil in the sight of the Lord and that he followed the sins of Jeroboam. One of Israel's cardinal sins was the worship of the calf, which King Joash to get rid of. Despite his willful disobedience to God's commandments, Elisha never gave up on him. This should be the commitment of longsuffering that spiritual fathers make to their sons in ministry in this day. Though the son may falter and misstep, the spiritual father should patiently and compassionately endure teaching the lessons which have to be learned by spiritual sons and daughters. Some lessons have to be learned through the harsh consequences of not taking heed to instruction. This was the case with King Joash. (Guzik, 2018).

Many young men and women are marked for greatness and success. Still, because of their unwillingness to submit to spiritual leadership and guidance, they find themselves falling short of their maximum potential. King Joash found himself in a challenging position. Although he was in power as the king, impending doom approaching from the King of Syria left the nation of Israel helpless and powerless.

> 2 Kings 13:14: *"Now Elisha was fallen sick of his sickness whereof he died. And Joash the king of Israel came down unto him, and wept over his face, and said, O my father, my father, the chariot of Israel, and the horsemen thereof."*

This is a powerful picture of a son who realized his desperate need for the guidance of a spiritual father. There were many times where King Joash disregarded the prophetic words that flowed from Elisha's lips. Still, when faced with the thought of Elisha's departure and Israel's impending doom, Joash became overwhelmed by the sobering reality. At that moment, he knew facing and overcoming a repressive enemy without his spiritual father was going to be impossible.

All too often, we fail to let the important people in our lives know how valuable they are. We wait until they are laid out in a casket with flowers strewn around them. Elisha is on his deathbed, down to his last breath, but like a spiritual father, he halted the dying process long enough to impart a prophetic word of deliverance to Joash on behalf of Israel. This impartation was words of instruction that would help determine Israel's future.

Elisha told King Joash to take the bow and arrows in his hands; this act in itself had more meaning than what young Joash knew (2 Kings 13:15-19). There were many times when I was given words of instruction that did not make a lot of sense. But as years have passed, I can see how those exact words were the difference makers in many of my outcomes.

Without any apparent hesitation, King Joash took hold of the bow and arrows as Elisha instructed him. There were no follow-up questions that were asked, like, *"Why are you asking me to pick up the bow and arrows?"* This shows the trust and confidence that Joash placed in Elisha's words. When instructions come without any revelation of the benefit to us, it leaves us in a place of uncertainty. We question the why, the what, the where, and the how. In a lot of cases, we observe how God communicated with His prophets, and we note that often instructions came without details:

> *"Elijah, go, get down to Zarephath, for there I have commanded a widow woman to sustain thee there"* (1 Kings 17:9).

> *"See, I have set thee over the nations, and over kingdoms, to root out, and to pull down, to destroy and to throw down, to build and to plant"* (Jeremiah 1:10).

Similarly, God uses Elisha to lay out some specific instructions to King Joash without sharing his actions' implications.

In 2000, God gave me a dream of a landscaper coming to my house to replace the sod in my front yard. I had no idea what this dream meant, but the meaning was slowly revealed in the coming weeks.

I was asked to preach at The Church of God International General Assembly. The afternoon before I preached, I was met by Bishop Selwyn Arnold, a man I deeply respect. He placed his hand on my shoulder and said, "You can do this." He must have perceived the trepidation and anxiety that I was experiencing —that touch and those words of affirmation gave me a surge of renewed confidence.

That night I preached the message, *Shoulder to Shoulder*, a theme that reverberated throughout the denomination even until today. Later that night, I received a call from the Church of God's Executive Committee asking me to accept an appointment in Southern New England as the Administrative Bishop. A response was required of me in a matter of hours. This was a grueling decision to make because it involved relocating my family over 1400 hundred miles north. It meant uprooting my wife from her job and deciding to leave the church I loved and knew God had called me to. It was that same night that the revelation of the dream became clear. Southern New England was the new sod that I had dreamed was being placed on my lawn.

I gathered my family together to discuss this new possibility. My daughter Ashley said something to me that removed all doubt from my mind about the decision to move. She said, *"If God is saying to go, you do what God said."* Her words at that moment gave me a sense of relief. This was the same sense of relief King Joash needed as he faced the uncertainties of the approaching conflict. Joash needed the touch of a spiritual father to prepare him for what was ahead.

Up to this point, Elisha has only been verbally involved, but the magnitude of the need propelled Elisha to become more tangibly involved. Elisha lays his hands on Joash's hands while King Joash gripped the bow and arrows (2 Kings 13:16). This is a powerful illustration of a spiritual father laying his hands on a spiritual son. A father's touch can have a remarkable impact on the life of a child.

One day as my father and I were driving through the city, he took his right hand and placed it on my shoulder. What appeared to be just another act of natural affection between father and son was elevated when he expressed how proud he was of me. The moment, though simple, was defining. It was a tangible demonstration of affirmation and support. At that moment, I resolved not ever to fail my father. This is what the touch of Elisha would also mean to Joash.

Regrettably, many fathers do not feel the need to be affectionate with their sons. In many circles, it is looked upon as unmasculine. In reality, our sons need to experience our touch; they need to feel our sense of affirmation. Some fathers are so disconnected from their families due to divorce, incarceration, and in some cases, they're just emotionally unavailable. This may sound like an anomaly, but in many children's lives, it is a reality.

One day one of my sons was having a real struggle and was facing a tremendous setback. Knowing words would not be enough, I hugged him. As I embraced him, I could see his face brighten up with hope and possibility. I don't fail to consider what would have been the outcome of that challenging experience for my son had I not been there to embrace him and give him the reassurance he needed. I am thankful for what that moment taught me and for the opportunity to share the impartation of what it taught me with my sons.

When Elisha placed his hand on King Joash's hand, it signaled spiritual strength on top of natural strength. Although King Joash had the commandership over an army of fighting soldiers, Elisha had been the voice of spiritual commandership and the voice of Israel. King Joash had youth and vitality on his side, whereas Elisha possessed spiritual wisdom and a charismatic spirit.

Envision this image of a dying Elisha, placing his feeble hand on the strong hand of King Joash. Elisha's hand could have never steadied the hand of King Joash for an accurate shot from the bow. It could not have made King Joash more efficient in the task that was before him. However, it did signal to King Joash that Elisha's God was with him. This is the message that we must continue to signal to our spiritual sons, which is, *as God has kept me, so will God keep you.* King Joash, the God of Elisha, can be your God.

I would like to make one more application out of this moment in King Joash's life. Elisha, *because of Joash's failures*, could have left him to his consequences. But the prophet recognized that there was a more significant gain at stake than personal grudges or personal feelings. The kingdom of Israel hung in the balance, so at that point, it was not about Elisha or Joash; it was about the assignment.

On many occasions, I have witnessed spiritual fathers fail to touch their sons in the very moments they needed it the most because of the father's pride and hurt. Maybe the son betrayed the father in some way. Jesus showed us an accurate picture of forgiveness when the prodigal son came home, and the father ran out to embrace, receive, and restore his son. This is what must continue to happen even with our spiritual children.

Spiritual sons also have a responsibility to honor and respect the fathers God has placed in their lives. They must not be withdrawn and unwilling to receive impartation when it comes. Today, many spiritual sons need to return to their father's home and humble themselves, just as many fathers need to allow their sons to return home and put pride aside.

I have seen this cyclical pattern repeatedly. Older men who have struggled to build up congregations or businesses are cast aside when their strength begins to wane—cast aside and discarded as though all they were and all they did before no longer mattered. I have seen spiritual sons take over and dismantle everything that their fathers had established, only to the detriment of the future of the ministry or business. We can learn from the mistakes of others and stop the cycle from repeating itself.

Elisha further instructs King Joash to open the window eastward. *"The window was opened eastward toward Syria and specifically toward Aphek, the most strategic site between Damascus and Samaria"* (2 Kings 13:17). It conveys that King Joash was focused on his target with precision. It is easy to become distracted, especially when you are close to your desired goal. Like King Joash, we have to come face-to-face with crisis moments that require a father's steady touch and become that which empowers us spiritually.

I recall taking on the new challenge of pastoring a culturally different church from any other church I had pastored in the past. Every new assignment comes with its own unique set of challenges and obstacles, but this one also came with detractors and doubters who watched and waited on me to fail. I found strength in those difficult moments from a spiritual father who I liken to Moses.

In Numbers Chapter 27, God instructs Moses to take Joshua before the congregation and lay his hands upon him. Moses laid his hands upon him. It was the symbolic act of bestowing Moses' honor upon him. It was done so that the people would submit to Joshua's authority.

> Numbers 27:22-23*: "And Moses did as the Lord commanded him: and he took Joshua, and set him before Eleazar, the priest, and before all the congregation: And he laid his hands upon him, and gave him a charge, as the Lord commanded by the hand of Moses."*

This is what I experienced in November 2011. There was no congregation watching; there was no paparazzi to take pictures and write articles about what was taking place. But at center stage where the former pastor and me. At that moment, Bishop Jocelyn Williams laid hands on me and spoke words of empowerment and confirmation into my life. He laid his hands on me, and he prayed spiritual vitality and faith into my inner man. Every time I have had doubts and moments of fear, I draw from that moment. When I visit him, I ask him to lay his hands on me and pray for me again.

With the void of spiritual fathers, too many sons miss the blessings bestowed upon them through the laying on of hands. The touch of a father can make a tremendous difference in the life of a struggling son who feels lost and weak in moments of adversity. Paul refers to a time when he had laid hands on young Timothy, providing him with the spiritual impartation that would carry him through the dark moments of ministry (2 Timothy 1:6).

Who could ever forget the 1992 Olympics in Barcelona, Spain? Derek Redmond was running but suddenly came up limping during the semi-final of the 400-meter race. It appeared tragic because he was projected to fare very well in that race. However, what at first seemed to be tragic turned into an emotionally exhilarating moment. Redmon got off the ground and willed himself around the track limping all the way, shrugging off any assistance from the attendants. His father bravely came from the sideline and grabbed his son's arm. With tears and clearly in anguishing pain, Redmon clung to his father's shoulders. With the father holding on to his son, and the son relying on the father for strength, Derek Redmon made it across the finish line to thunderous applause from the crowd. There is no more poignant depiction of the power of a father's touch. Redmond was able to finish the race because of the impact of his father's touch. That touch gave him the courage to overcome what might have been a physical impossibility.

Elisha told Joash to point the arrow toward the target and shoot, and Elisha declared, *"The arrow of the Lord's deliverance from Syria"*

(2 Kings 13:17). This prophetic statement indicated to Joash that the Lord would give him victory in the battle over his enemy. An enemy that plagued the children of Israel for many years was now going to be overcome by the armies of the Lord. What was even more telling for Joash was that the victory was going to come by his hands, the same hands Elisha had touched.

At that moment, it did not matter how weak Elisha might have been. His spiritual intuitiveness and wisdom were all that King Joash needed in that hour. It is essential that we do not discount the contribution that spiritual parents can make in helping to guide this next generation into their destiny.

The next thing Elisha tells Joash to do was important but more important was how the young man chose to carry out the instruction. Elisha tells Joash to take the arrows in his hand and strike the ground with them. The Bible says that Joash hit the ground three times and stopped. Elisha became angry because it would appear that Joash did not take the assignment as seriously as he should have. Elisha scolded King Joash and said, "*If you had only struck the ground five or six times, you would have destroyed the Syrians*" (2 Kings 13:19). Young Joash held the destiny and fate of a people in his hands, but in his response, he forfeited the ability to obliterate his enemy.

This is called a missed opportunity. It was a moment in time that Joash could never recover. How often do we fail to seize opportunities because we fail to execute in moments that can change the course of our future? We have missed opportunities to start a business, write a book, take a promotion on the job; connect with the right person in marriage; to move forward in the ministry God has called us to do. Moments of hesitation can lead to a lifetime of losses. For Joash, it was a failure by omission.

In his moment of failure, we see the wisdom of a spiritual father, Elisha, speaking words of correction to Joash. A father's inability to correct his sons always leads to the ensnarement of his sons.

Please consider Eli, who had the opportunity to correct his sons, Phinehas and Hophni, but because he failed to do so, it caused them to die prematurely (1 Samuel 2:34). Many ministries have been cut short of their potential because of the absence of spiritual fathers who were courageous enough to correct their sons.

> Proverbs 19:18: *"Chasten thy son while there is hope and let not thy soul spare for his crying."*
>
> Proverbs 19:18: *"Discipline your children, for in that there is hope; do not be a willing party to their death."*

Elisha, with the heart of a father, did not allow the moment to close without his words of correction; failing to do so could have resulted in tragedy. When a son hears not only the words of a father's discipline but the heart of a father who loves him despite his mistakes, it challenges the son to pursue his divine purpose with more vigilance.

I recall another interaction I had with my father. I had done something that displeased him. He sat me down, placed his hand on my shoulder, and spoke to me sternly. I was hurt by some things he said, but in the end, I knew that what he said was true. I also knew that he cared about my destiny, and he did not want to see me fail continuously. He said, *"I am saying these things to you because I love you, and I tell you these things because I want to see you go further than I have gone."*

Many spiritual sons and daughters need to hear this today. I want to thank God for spiritual parents who touched my life in so many ways. I am speaking of the late Bishop Jonathan Ramsey Sr. and Mother Evelyn Ramsey. Their faith, courage, wisdom, and commitment will always be landmarks that will remain with me all the days of my life.

Proverbs 22:28: *"Remove not the ancient landmark, which thy fathers have set."*

My parents were examples of servant leadership, individuals who had a genuine heart for ministry. It was never about promotions, prosperity, and prominence. My parents received a lot of accolades and applause, but their legacy is one of selfless ministry.

On one occasion, as Christmas was approaching, my father called the family together to explain how we would share our gifts with members of the church he pastored at the time. What touched my heart so deeply was that my father drove over two hours away to church every Sunday and some weekdays, and now he was willing to give even more of himself, not only his time but also his substance for the kingdom.

At this time, my father was pastoring in Stuart, Florida, which was a developing community but very impoverished. That Christmas, the people saw Christ in action and not just in words. My parents not only touched our lives with their altruistic nature but the community of Stuart, Florida, at large. Many of those households that our family gave to did not have fathers in the home, but they received a father's touch Christmas. We have a tremendous opportunity today as spiritual parents to impact our children's lives and the next generation of children who may not otherwise experience a father's touch.

Chapter 5

Absence of a Father's Presence

As I walked through a neighborhood Walmart, I noticed one of the attendants running toward a man rolling a shopping cart out of the door. The man's shopping cart was filled with items that the man could not afford.

The real tragedy was that a little boy about five years old was sitting in the cart as his father attempted to defraud the store. The attendant shouted, *"What kind of example are you to your son?"* Too often, this is the image our children are left with when fathers fail to be the role models their children desire them to be. The idea of a father's failure is even more haunting in the child's life when the father is missing in action.

It is common knowledge that mothers share a powerful connection with their unborn child while the child develops in her womb. From the time the baby is conceived in the womb, an embryonic bond is formed. It is much more than just the baby being fed and nurtured in the mother's womb; there is an emotional connection that takes place, and that connection continues throughout the entire incubation period.

The developing fetus is aware of the mother's heartbeat and voice and can respond to touch or movement. By the seventh month of pregnancy, two-thirds of women report having a strong maternal bond with their unborn child. In 2010, author Paul Raeburn wrote an article discussing the vital role a father plays in the physical and emotional health of the unborn child.

> *"Infants whose fathers were absent— and was not involved in the pregnancy— were more likely to be born with lower birth weight and to be born prematurely. The death rate of infants whose fathers were not around was nearly four times greater than that of infants whose fathers were involved"* (Raeburn, 2010).

> *"Regardless of race or ethnicity, the neonatal death rate of father-absent infants was nearly four times that of their counterparts with involved fathers"* (Alia, 2010).

I have had the privilege of sitting down with many young men who were incarcerated for extended periods. Many of them would recount stories of how they felt abandoned by their fathers, and for some, that abandonment stemmed from not even knowing who their fathers were. As I listened to each story, I heard one common reoccurring theme: Each young man, in his unique way, would attribute his poor choices to the absence of a positive male role model.

There is a growing crisis in the United States. According to the U S. Census Bureau, 19.7 million children, which translates to more than 1 in 4 children, live without a father in the home (U.S. Census Bureau, 2020).

Consequently, the *father factor issue* is at the root of all societal ills in the United States. According to research, when a child is raised in a home void of a father's presence, they face the increased probability of the following: poverty, behavioral disturbances, incarceration, teen pregnancy, and child abuse, *to list a few.*

The fullness of challenges unleashed on societies by paternal absenteeism is too many to list in this book alone. In addition to the research available through secular institutions, the Bible also presents us with case studies that highlight this topic.

One example of this is the relationship between King David and his favorite son Absalom. Their relationship exposes some of the pitfalls caused by disconnections in father-son relationships. Absalom's name has now become synonymous with discontentment, rebellion, and self-destruction. The name Absalom means the father of peace, but as the story of Absalom's life unfolds, it reveals overtones of everything except peace.

The disconnect is between father and son begins when Absalom discovers that his half-brother Amnon has violated his sister Tamar. It not only brought shame to David's family but the entire nation of Israel. Animosity and contempt for Amnon grew as Absalom watched his sister Tamar mourn the loss of her virginity and finds herself faced with a life of disgrace. Absalom devises a plan to take revenge on his brother Amnon and avenge his sister's honor. He prepares a feast and summons all of his brothers to take part in the festivities—this setup for revenge results in a polarizing domino effect.

Many sons are behind bars, standing on corners, being moved from one foster home to the next; others work in factories where they feel trapped in careers they hate. There are also some young men and women sitting in corporate offices, dealing with the internal wounds of anger. Though others around them may dismiss their pain as unbridled hostility, their inner scars are real. One underlying reason for anger and frustration stems from the longing for attention, the need to acknowledge the issues that are plaguing one's life.

We see this very issue in the life of Absalom. Absalom sat day-by-day harboring intense feelings of hatred for his brother Amnon. It would appear on the surface that there was no justice for Tamar. King David knew about the events that had transpired but failed to take the initiative to bring discipline to Amnon for his actions.

In Second Samuel 13:21, David was furious, but his anger never addressed the problem before him. Some biblical commentators believe that David's moral guilt restrained him from having the courage to reprimand Amnon. A father's sins came back to haunt him. How many sons are forced to stand by in silence as countless acts of violence and abuse are perpetrated against those they love?

David's inaction becomes the torch that lights the flame of Absalom's desire to take revenge against his brother. The Bible says Absalom said neither anything good nor bad toward his brother Amnon while plotting against him. It would appear anger had subsided to the outside world, but there were thoughts of murder and revenge beneath the surface.

Ralph Waldo Emerson said, *"For every minute you remain angry, you give up sixty seconds of peace of mind."*

James 1:20, *NIV* says, *"For man's anger does not bring about the righteous life that God desires."* Anger becomes a destructive weapon that brings about disaster for the individual that carries it and for everything and everyone that lies in its pathway. Unbridled anger is equivalent to a deadly tornado that carves its way through cities leaving destruction and devastation.

Absalom festered in anger for two years until his plot of revenge was ready for implementation. Absalom then seeks permission from his father, King David, to invite his brothers to a festival of sheepshearers. Since King David has no action to punish Amnon, Absalom takes matters into his own hands. The negligence of one generation creates havoc and disaster in another. When problems arise, silence and inaction are never the answer.

Absalom with his servants waits patiently until Ammon becomes inebriated and then kills him. David's failure to act on the first violation causes the second violation (*Absalom murdering his brother)* to be even more damaging and egregious.

> *"Never do anything when you are in a temper, for you will do everything wrong."*

"One should not lose one's temper unless one is certain of getting angrier and angrier to the end."

"Speak when you are angry, and you will make the best speech you will ever regret."

"Whatever is begun in anger ends in shame." William Butler Yeats

ISOLATION

David is immediately informed of Absalom's act and is only alleviated that only Amnon is killed and not his other sons. The Bible says that King David, his sons, and his servants wept very bitterly. Absalom fled and remained away from Jerusalem. Although he longed for Absalom's presence, David did not go to his son. David had failed to execute punishment for Amnon for his vile act on Tamar, and now there was no disciplinary action taken against Absalom for his sin against Amnon. When a son is left to his purposes, destructive behavior will most often be the result. What kind of pain and hurt could have possibly been avoided had David sought to correct the behaviors of his sons?

Proverbs 13:24: *"Whosoever spares the rod hates his son, but he who loves him is diligent to discipline him"* (ESV).

Parents today may feel that discipline drives children away when discipline is a protective barrier that keeps evil things out while creating a safe and thriving haven within. Discipline provides our children with structure and boundaries; it communicates a message of care and love. David had the power and ability to chastise both Amnon and Absalom, and his failure to do so left tragedy in its tracks. Our Heavenly Father does not leave us to ourselves, but because He loves us, He chastens us.

> Hebrews 12:6: *"For whom the Lord loveth he chasteneth, and scourgeth every son whom he receiveth."*

> Proverbs 3:12: *"For whom the Lord loveth he correcteth; even as a father the son in whom he delighteth."*

When I was about 12 years old, I remember my father admonishing me about the importance of remaining in the sanctuary during service. On one particular Sunday, there was an accident that took place outside the church. The accident involved a young man who had lost control of his motorcycle. Everyone who had seen the accident stood and watched as first responders worked to assess and gain control of the situation.

You guessed it, out of curiosity, I followed the crowd. When my father heard what I had done, he immediately took me down the street to my grandmother's house and gave me a spanking that I will never forget. I knew that his response was out of his desire to protect me and his fear of what could have possibly happened to me as a spectator. You can believe that I got the message and never left church again during service, no matter what happened outside.

A father's discipline is a deterrent to a child's mischief. David's failure to act became the beginning of Absalom's continued destructive behavior. Maybe it was in David's thoughts that banishment would be an opportunity for Absalom to come to grips with his actions, but that would prove not to be the case.

Joab, the nephew of David, the commander of David's army, perceiving the depth of David's desire to be reunited with his son, devised a plan to bring Absalom back to Jerusalem. The plan worked, and King David requested that Joab bring Absalom back to Jerusalem:

> 2 Samuel 14:21: *"And the king said unto Joab, behold now, I have done this thing: go therefore, bring the young man Absalom again."*

On April 30, 1975, many sons came home from Vietnam after 20 years of sacrificing their families, futures, and even their own lives. A significant number of them felt rejected, unappreciated, disgraced, and abandoned by the very nation they went to defend. Some came home with medical conditions that made them unemployable. Others came home with post-traumatic stress disorders due to traumas endured during service. Others even developed addictions to drugs and alcohol.

I can vividly remember seeing pictures of people picketing during the Vietnam War—*bring our sons home*! But when they came home, there was nowhere for most of them to go; today, we can see elements of the same dynamic repeated, men feeling isolated and abandoned by those they believe should have supported them.

INSURRECTION

David would find himself in danger after bringing Absalom back home would be that of David's own doing. Rather than Absalom's absence bringing peace, it bred a spirit of contempt and rebellion. The son that David thought of as his heir apparent now became a thorn in David's side. Rather than David grooming a successor, he created an insurrectionist.

Before bringing Absalom back to Jerusalem, David gave Joab specific instructions. Parts of those instructions were that Absalom could not see David's face. It was almost as if a father was turning his back on his son. Isolation was not enough; now Absalom had to wrestle with the thought of rejection and abandonment. It may have been the most critical time in Absalom's life. David had an opportunity to teach Absalom life lessons about the destructiveness of untamed anger but instead placed him in a position of isolation.

Let's take a look at the spirit of rebellion in its formidable stages. The Bible says there was none praised like Absalom in all of Israel for his good looks, from the sole of his foot to the crown of his head. No blemish was found in him; even his hair was a point of great focus and admiration.

Joseph Benson Commentary says, *"In those days hair was accounted a great ornament, and the longer it was, the more it was esteemed"* (Benson, 1857).

Matthew Henry Commentary says, *"Nothing is said of*

Absalom's wisdom and piety. All there is said of him is that he was a very handsome man. A poor commendation for a man that had nothing else in him valuable" (Henry, 1997).

Absalom lived in Jerusalem for two years without the affirmation or affection of his father. Silence speaks volumes, especially when you are left to speculate what silence means. For Absalom, it must have expressed displeasure, disconnection, discontentment, and disdain. The absence was painful enough, but now to add to Absalom's growing contempt, the horror of David's silence.

We can see contempt in the actions of Absalom that followed. Deception, betrayal, and presumption would all describe the actions of Absalom. His behavior was the result of David's inability to make a spiritual connection with his son. He, in all his pride, would eventually and methodically attempt to overthrow David as king. The tragedy of this spirit of rebellion was that it came from someone from David's household, his flesh and blood, someone that was fed at the king's table.

It is no wonder why this story ends tragically. We can see evidence of this same spirit in the business world, in Hollywood, and even in the Church, where someone wants to seek out power by any means necessary.

By the time David realized the depth of the problem he had created, his primary counselor, Ahithophel, had been brought into allegiance with Absalom.

> 2 Samuel 15:12-13: *"And Absalom sent for Ahithophel the Gilonite, David's counselor, from his city, even from Giloh, while he offered sacrifices. And the conspiracy was strong, for the people increased continually with Absalom. And there came a messenger to David, saying, the hearts of the men of Israel are after Absalom."*

The insurrection became so great that it forced David to flee the city of Jerusalem. Here we have a picture of a father being pursued by the son he loved, but now anger and vengeance have usurped their relationship. Absalom, at one time, probably longed for the direction and correction that only a father could provide. But when he saw that his father chose to be absent, it allowed that longing to be turned to animosity and contempt. As great a king as David was, he failed miserably as a father in many aspects.

In the midst of all of our significant accomplishments and awards, one of the most remarkable statements that could be said of any man is, "You are a good father." I have heard it said too many times of many great leaders that while they won the world for Jesus, they lost their families due to continual absence. I vowed that I would never want that said of me.

Absalom's anger and resentment toward his father became his undoing. Absalom failed to see his own three children because he allowed bitterness to drive him to a destructive end. While pursuing his father, Absalom's mule runs under the bough of a tree, and he, in turn, finds himself hanging by his beautiful long hair. Joab, the captain of David's army finishes the job by taking three darts and thrusting them through the heart of Absalom.

> 2 Samuel 18:23: *"And the king was much moved and went up to the chamber over the gate and wept; and as he went, thus he said. O my son Absalom, my son, my son, Absalom would God I had died for thee, O Absalom, my son, my son!"*

What if Absalom had known the depth of his father's love for him? The loss of his life could not be recovered, much like the absence of his father's presence could not be undone.

We see this drama played out in many settings in our modern society. Men with great promise fail to reach the pinnacle of their potential because the absence of a father becomes the destructive weapon that destroys them. It is incumbent upon us as fathers to be present in our children's lives and not allow our absence to become the weapons that form against them.

Chapter 6

Absence of a Righteous Voice

Psalm 34:17: "*The righteous cry and the Lord hears and delivereth them out of all their troubles.*"

In the age that we live in, our world desperately searches for righteous voices that will declare God's truth to a rapidly deteriorating culture into godlessness. The Bible says, "*Righteousness exalteth a nation and sin is a reproach to any people*" (Proverbs 14:34). God's word's fulfilled, indicating the imminent return of the Lord. For this cause, we must have spiritual fathers who can stand in integrity and be a beacon of light for the masses fumbling in the darkness.

When I was growing up, I would often hear sermons about the coming of the Lord. Bible study classes would teach on what to expect in the last days. It was common to listen to songs like *"Signs of the Judgment Now."* and *"Get Right Church, Let's Go Home."* I recall hearing sermons entitled, *"Prepare to meet thy God," "Do Not Let It Be Said," "Too late,"* and *"Tomorrow May Never Come."* Even now, these messages reverberate in my ears, reminding me that my life must be in accordance with God's Word and that I must always remain prepared for His return.

The most popular sermons that preached focus today on themes that encourage people to "live their best life now," prosperity, health, fitness, and financial freedom. Though I agree with the tenor of all of these messages, I also believe these types of messages must be undergirded with the foundational message of salvation and walking in obedience to God's Word. Some of the voices of spiritual fathers that once kept our focus on Jesus Christ have either gone on to their eternal reward, while others silenced. The demand for "feel good" messages has led many to believe that sermons concerning the Lord's return are antiquated and no longer relevant to the times we live.

More recently, we have seen many religious leaders becoming more active in the political arena, even to the point of basing the entire foundation of their ministry on issues like social justice, women's rights, and a lot more. This loss of eternal focus has caused many people in society to take a second look at the Church and question if the Church is fulfilling the mandates of the Word of God.

I thank God for ministers like Billy Graham, E. V. Hill, Bishop George Wallace, John Osteen, and the many others who were mighty trumpets that sounded the alarm of righteousness and holiness. My concern for this generation is that voices like these are far and few. The Word of God has become diluted, and the ministry has been infiltrated by preachers who seek out stardom and fame more than the building up of God's Kingdom.

> 2 Timothy 4:1-5: *"I charge thee therefore before God, and the Lord Jesus Christ, who shall judge the quick and the dead at his appearing and his kingdom; Preach the word; be instant in season, out of season;*

> *reprove, rebuke, exhort with all longsuffering and doctrine. For the time will come when they will not endure sound doctrine; but after their own lusts shall they heap to themselves teachers, having itching ears; And they shall turn away their ears from the truth, and shall be turned unto fables. But watch thou in all things, endure afflictions, do the work of an evangelist, make full proof of thy ministry."*

Paul instructs a young pastor, Timothy, to be on guard in the last days against people who will desire pastors and teachers who will soothe their ears and dull their consciences by providing the people with what they want rather than what they need. Sadly, this is prevalent now. Today, we have preachers who are more technically polished than their predecessors but fail at holiness, purity, and righteousness. Practical application of the Word of God is the answer to the many issues that plague the lives of today's congregants. While providing practical teaching, there must also be a righteous voice to this generation.

From the beginning of creation, man has found himself in constant rebellion against the will and purpose of God. We see this in the first man, Adam. God provides Adam with every good tree of the garden but instructs him not to partake of one, the tree of the knowledge of good and evil. God said to Adam, *"For the day you eat of that tree you shall surely die*" (Genesis 2:17).

When Adam and Eve ate of that tree, they did not immediately physically die, but they cut themselves off from the unrestricted presence of God. The perfect communion and fellowship that man once enjoyed with his maker were now lost.

Despite man's failure, God has continuously sought to restore what sin caused a man to forfeit. Due to one man's actions, sin came into the world, but the redeeming feature is that redemption has brought about redemption for humanity through one man, Christ. The Psalmist David asked a profound question in Psalm 8:4-5, *"What is man that thou art mindful of him? The son of man that thou visit him? For thou hast made him a little lower than the angels, and thou hast crowned him with glory and honor."* God could have separated himself from man forever, but instead, He chooses to pursue man by raising up righteous voices to carry out His divine plan on the earth.

After Adam and Eve's rebellious act, their son Cain becomes envious of his brother Abel's offering, which God delights. Cain's jealousy would eventually drive him to murder his brother. The Bible says God did not have respect for Cain's offering. Some theologians assert that the reason God accepted Abel's offering and rejected Cain's offering was that Abel gave his best to the Lord, while Cain gave less than his best. Other theologians conclude that Abel's gift was accepted because he gave his gift from a pure heart of worship, while Cain's offering was rejected because his gift was a symbol of careless worship. God seeks people who will worship Him in spirit and truth.

Ever since the fall of man through Adam, no act of rebellion has had the power to negate God's eternal plan of salvation for man. Genesis 4:25 says, *"Adam knew Eve again and Eve conceived and they called his name Seth."* The name Seth means compensation, appointed, and anointed. Seth became the righteous seed that replaced Abel in the earth. Through Seth, men began to call on the name of the Lord again.

God's original plan has always been to have a relationship with man. One such person who accomplished this was Enoch. The Bible does not provide us a lot of information about Enoch, but from what we know, he was the son of Jared, who the Bible says was one hundred and sixty years old when he had Enoch. He lived another eight hundred years and had sons and daughters. We also know that Enoch lived on earth for 365 years. Enoch was the father of Methuselah, who was the oldest man that ever lived. When Methuselah died, he was 969 years old. It is important because the same year that Methuselah died, the flood came upon the earth. The name Methuselah means *"the man of the dart"* or *"he shall send his death"* or, more provocatively, *"when he is dead, it shall be sent."*

Genesis 6:5-7 records the following concerning life prior to the flood:

> *"And God saw that the wickedness of man was great in the earth, and that every imagination of the thoughts of his heart was only evil continually. And it repented the Lord that he had made man on the earth, and it grieved him at his heart. And the Lord said, I will destroy man whom I have created from the face of the earth; both man, and beast, and the creeping thing, and the fowls of the air; for it repenteth me that I have made them."*

There was gross wickedness upon the earth, so much so that it grieved God that He ever created man.

> *"Wickedness had filled the earth so that the thoughts of the heart and of man was evil continually"* (Genesis 6:5).

This is a very dark and gloomy description of what was happening on the earth at the time. Enoch predates the flood by 1,064 years. The Bible gives us a clear picture of what appears to be the collapse of morals in the people after Enoch was translated.

Enoch was a righteous voice to his generation. The Bible says that Enoch walked with God and then disappeared because he was translated—meaning he did not die physically. That word righteous denotes godly character and moral purity. Righteousness is the quality or state of being morally correct and justifiable. It can be considered synonymous with "rightness" or being "upright."

> Proverbs 14:34: *"Righteousness exalteth a nation: but sin is a reproach to any people."*

In every generation, there is the need for someone to be the mouthpiece of God, crying out for righteousness. Many people down through the years have been a voice of righteousness for their time. Enoch walked before God in such integrity and purity that his name is mentioned among the heroes of faith.

> Hebrews 11:5: *"By faith Enoch was translated that he should not see death; and was not found, because God had translated him: for before*

his translation he had this testimony, that he pleased God."

Enoch was a man who walked in righteousness, a man of faith, a man of prayer, and a man of consecration. This testimony of Enoch's life must have caught the attention of the community around him. A man who walks in communion with God is a man who is passionate in his worship, fervent in his love for God, and focused on doing the will of God.

Communion is defined as the exchanging of intimate thoughts and feelings. It is particularly true when the exchange is on a mental or spiritual level. In a spiritual sense, communion can be described as being in constant communication with God. To have communion with God is to walk in union and harmony with God. Enoch took delight in being in the presence of God.

Imagine the fact that a holy God took notice of the life of his creation in such a way that his walk with God became the vehicle of his translation into the very presence of God. Enoch's worship experience with God became who he was. Enoch's life was an example of the transforming power of true worship. There was no distinction between who he was outside and within the act of ceremonial worship.

2 Corinthians 5:17: *"Therefore if any man be in Christ, he is a new creature: old things are passed away: behold, all things are become new."*

Enoch's covenant with God was evident even in the naming of his son, Methuselah. As previously stated, the name Methuselah means *"the man of the dart."* Other translations of the name are *"he shall send death"* and *"when he is dead, he shall send death."* Some theologians say that Methuselah's name is an indication that God had made a covenant with Enoch that He would not allow the destruction of man to come until after his son was dead. Some scholars say (according to the Masoretic and Samaritan text), some scholars say that this name was given to Methuselah by a prophecy revealed to Enoch, indicating that destruction was coming to the land. The case for this assertion can easily be made, especially knowing the fact that precisely the same year that Methuselah died, the flood came upon the earth.

We can see through this covenant that God had great mercy and compassion on humanity. 1 Peter 3:20 says, *"Which sometime were disobedient, when once the longsuffering of God waited in the days of Noah, while the ark was a preparing, wherein few, that is eight souls were saved by water."* This verse of scripture was fulfilled in the days of Methuselah. God suffers long with man's wickedness and unwillingness to repent and turn toward Him.

Peter again reminds us of the mercy of God in 2 Peter 3:9:

"The Lord is not slack concerning his promise, as some men count slackness; but longsuffering to usward, not willing that any should perish, but that all should come to repentance."

Through the covenant that God made with Enoch, we can see the great lengths our God will go to redeem and restore us to

Himself. God is looking for righteous voices that will come to Him with submitted hearts, voices of those who are willing to be the moral conscience of a generation that has turned away from Him.

Enoch was that type of man. The Bible says Enoch had a testimony that his ways pleased God (Hebrews 12:5). Could it be possible that Enoch's walk before God caused God to reveal to him His divine will and plan? It seems to be what took place during the time that Enoch spent on earth. Enoch had a covenant promise from God. We know a covenant to be a binding agreement between parties. God's covenant with Enoch was generational because it not only spoke to his time but to the days of his son, Methuselah. God always honors His Word. Methuselah died before the flood came upon the earth.

There is a quote in the book of Jude that comes from one of the lost books of the Bible, with Enoch ascribed as the author. The Book of Enoch was among the books of the Bible that were not canonized. However, theologians say though the Book of Enoch in its entirety does not fall under the category of being inspired, words quoted from the book of Enoch are contained in the Book of Jude, which makes them inspired.

> Jude 1:14-15: *"And Enoch also, the seventh from Adam, prophesied of these, saying, Behold, the Lord cometh with ten thousand of his saints, To execute judgment upon all, and to convince all that are ungodly among them of all their ungodly deeds which they have ungodly committed, and of all their hard speeches which ungodly sinners have*

spoken against him."

Just as prophesied in Methuselah's name, the judgment of God came on the earth, destroying all of creation except Noah, his family, and the animals that entered the ark.

Enoch lived on earth (365 years) was brief compared to others who lived during his time. Nevertheless, what Enoch experienced in his lifetime set him apart. Enoch walked with God and was not (Genesis 5:24). Hours after Enoch's translation, family and friends alike must have been asking where Enoch disappeared to? Through oral and written tradition, Enoch was translated up to God. To be translated means to be transferred, relocated, and to be transported into the place of God.

Can you imagine walking with God on such a level of communion and covenant relationship that one day while walking in that fellowship, you are suddenly taken away, caught up in the presence of God? Enoch experienced the hope of every Believer—the hope to be found so faithful to God's Word that we too will be caught away to our eternal reward forever to be in the presence of the Lord.

> 1 Thessalonians 4:16-17: *"For the Lord himself shall descend from heaven with a shout, with the voice of the archangel, and with the trump: and the dead in Christ shall rise first: Then we which are alive and remain shall be caught up together with them in the clouds, to meet the Lord in the air: and so shall we ever be with the Lord."*

Let us consider another righteous voice that spoke to his generation, and that is Father Abraham. Abraham was willing to leave his father's house and everything that he had become accustomed to as an act of obedience to the call of God. And because of Abraham's obedience, God knew He could trust Abraham with an evangelistic assignment.

Abraham got a visitation from angels in the form of men. Their assignment was to go down and destroy Sodom and Gomorrah because of the wickedness in those cities. The Lord said, "*Shall I hide from Abraham what I am doing?*" What a testimony of Abraham's friendship with God, that God would take time to reveal to him the pending destruction that He was about to bring to the people of those cities.

Genesis 18:20-21: *"And the Lord said, because the cry of Sodom and Gomorrah is great, and because their sin is very grievous; I will go down now, and see whether they have done altogether according to the cry of it, which is come unto me; and if not, I will know."*

As the two men and Abraham proceed toward Sodom and Gomorrah, Abraham offers a prayer of intercession for the righteous who might be destroyed with the wicked people in Sodom and Gomorrah. Perhaps it was the knowledge that his nephew. Lot had decided to live in Sodom and Gomorrah. Abraham's plea begins with, "*God, if there be fifty righteous within the city, will you not spare it for the righteous in the city*" (Genesis 18:24).

There are tremendous implications of mercy and grace that these words are hinged. If there be 50, maybe they can turn back the darkness that now saturates the city. In our current day, I believe God still desires a people who will stand up for righteousness and lend their voices for the redemption of the land.

> Second Chronicles 7:14: *"If my people, which are called by my name, shall humble themselves, and pray, and seek my face, and turn from their wicked ways; then will I hear from heaven, and will forgive their sin, and will heal their land."*

The sad indictment against the people of Sodom and Gomorrah was that there were not 50 righteous souls found in the city. As Abraham continued his request to God, his numbers dwindled to 10, yet there were still not enough righteous people found to save the city.

What took place during Abraham's day is a warning to our generation today. God calls on the Church, the people of God, the righteous generation, to recognize the times and awaken out of sleep. There is a desperate need for spiritual fathers to take their place and be the much-needed righteous voices on the earth in this hour.

Because of Abraham's continued plea, Lot and his family were spared though Sodom and Gomorrah were destroyed. One righteous voice can alter the course of history for a family caught amid degradation and moral decay.

Psalm 34:17: *"The righteous cry, and the Lord heareth, and delivereth*

> *them out of all their troubles."*

Like Enoch and Abraham, Elijah was a righteous voice to his generation. The name Elijah means *"Yahweh is my God."* It connotes that God is my only God.

In the days of Elijah, Israel was under the evil leadership of King Ahab and Queen Jezebel. It was an unholy alliance. Under their leadership, Israel turned their back on God to worship the god Baal.

"As such, Baal was designated the universal god of fertility, and in that capacity, his title was Prince, Lord of the Earth. He was also called the Lord of Rain and Dew, the two forms of moisture that were indispensable for fertile soil in Canaan" (Britannica, 2020).

Rather than looking to God Almighty as their source, they sought after powerless idols of man's creation.

> Psalm 135:16-18: *"They have mouths, but they speak not; eyes have they, but they see not; They have ears, but they hear not; neither is there any breath in their mouths. They that make them are like unto them: so is everyone that trusteth in them."*

It was Elijah's assignment to be the righteous voice that would call the people of Israel back to the true and living God. Elijah had to be willing to put his life at risk to call a nation to a place of repentance. Because Israel rejected God, God shut up the heavens for three and a half years. There was no rain. Whereas there was a spiritual drought in Israel, there was now also a drought for water.

Rejecting an opportunity to repent, the people of Israel continued to follow after Baal. By the time Elijah spoke to the people, there were 450 prophets of Baal and 400 other prophets of the groves.

Elijah challenged the people of Israel to choose a side. He challenged them, saying, *"How long do you halt between two opinions? If you are going to serve God, serve God, but if you are going to serve Baal, serve Baal"* (1 Kings 18:21).

The Prophet Elijah called for a contest on Mount Carmel. He said, *"Let the God that answers by fire be the true God and let us worship Him"* (1 Kings 18:24). Elijah's righteous voice stood alone in the face of 850 false prophets, but God was with him.

The Prophets of Baal chose their bullock, cut it in pieces, lay it on the wood, and began praying to their God to bring down fire from heaven. Though they cried and cut themselves from morning to midday, no fire came down. Elijah asked the prophets of Baal in jest, *"Is your God asleep? Has your God taken a vacation?"* (1 Kings 18:27). Elijah was so confident in his God that he began to humiliate the prophets of Baal because of their futility.

However, when Elijah's turn came to call down fire from Heaven, the Bible says he broke down the altar and began to rebuild the altar (1 Kings 18:30). Just as Elijah did, we, too, need to reconstruct our altars and fall on our faces, and cry out to God in repentance so that He might again send the rain of His anointing, grace, and divine favor.

After Elijah rebuilt the altar, he dressed the altar placing 12 stones representative of the 12 tribes of Israel around the altar. Elijah cut the bullock into pieces and laid them on the wood. Elijah had a trench built around the altar and finally had four buckets of water poured on the sacrifice (1 Kings 18:32-33). As the people drew near to Elijah and the altar, Elijah cried out to the Lord God of Abraham, Isaac, and Israel.

> 1 Kings 18:37-38: *"Hear me, O Lord, hear me, that this people may know that thou art the Lord God, and that thou hast turned their heart back again. Then the fire of the Lord fell, and consumed the burnt sacrifice, and the wood, and the stones, and the dust, and licked up the water that was in the trench."*

When the people of Israel saw the miracle of the fire consuming not only the sacrifice but also licking up the water around the sacrifice, with one voice, they said, "*The Lord, he is the God*" (1 Kings 18:39b).

One man willing to stand up and be a righteous voice to a nation caused revival and restoration to come to a people. What would happen today if we had more righteous voices willing to cry out loud? *"Cry loud, spare not, lift up thy voice like a trumpet, and shew my people their transgression, and the house of Jacob their sins"* (Isaiah 58:1). We need spiritual fathers who are willing to lend their righteous voices as catalysts to stir extraordinary change in every stratum of our society.

Chapter 7

Absence of a Righteous Seed

A generation is emerging on the horizon, and they are unique from any generation before them. I call them "the more generation" because they will experience more, seek more, and do more; they will be more innovative and technologically savvy. They are adventurous and courageous—a generation that will not accept the status quo's limitations and ideals.

There is evidence of our children growing wiser and becoming more skilled all around us. Today's toddlers navigate complex cellphones, tablets, and computers with ease. While we are aware of their possibilities and potential to accomplish astronomical feats, there is still a danger that lurks and awaits them from the tempter himself. A seducing voice is calling them from the darkness that seeks to destroy them before they ever have the opportunity to reach the heights of their full potential.

> John 10:10: *"The thief cometh not, but for to steal, and to kill, and to destroy I am come that they might have life, and that they might have it more abundantly."*

Though greatness may be ahead for this generation, some vices and snares have been cunningly set up and specifically devised to cause them to mire in humiliation and despair. The Church has been given the tremendous responsibility to help the next generation avoid the traps before them. We have been given the mandate to point them in the direction of their God-ordained purpose and destiny.

As I converse with this emerging generation, the continuous pleas I hear from them are, *"Give me a chance," "Do not count me out when I make mistakes," "I have something to offer," "See my potential and not my past."* This generation constantly searches for their purpose; they are confident of their giftings and talents but are desperately unsure of where they fit in. The Church must answer the defining question: *Are we ready to embrace this fiery, sometimes impulsive, potential-filled generation?*

This generation has the energy and strength to move the needle in the continued spiritual combat against Satan. The enemy is threatened by the possibilities of what they can achieve for the kingdom of God. For this reason, we see the enemy unleashing every possible strategy and tool he can to silence and immobilize this generation.

> Joel 2:28-29: *"And it shall come to pass afterward, that I will pour out my spirit upon all flesh; and your sons and your daughters shall prophesy, your old men shall dream dreams, your young men shall see visions. And also upon the servants and upon the handmaids in those days will I pour out my spirit."*

God has a promise that overrides and disannuls its accomplishment for every plot and plan that Satan has for this generation. The spiritual fathers of today must continuously speak the message of promise and fulfillment of promise over the lives and into the hearing of this generation.

> Matthew 11:12: *"And from the days of John the Baptist until now the kingdom of heaven suffereth violence and the violent take it by force."*

Many young people are searching for their identity; they are yet to discover their self-worth and value to the kingdom of God.

Gideon, the fifth judge of Israel, who was from the tribe of Manasseh, had a similar challenge. Gideon was poised for greatness but found himself a victim of Israel's plight. In Gideon's time, the Israelites were under the bondage of the Midianites. During this period, the Midianites ravished the Israelites, their territories, and their harvest seasonally. Israel was in a position of fear and retreat, hiding in caves and the mountains. It was at this time God visited Gideon while he was hiding from the Midianites by the winepress. Gideon was threshing wheat, trying to keep it hidden from the Midianites, when the angel of the Lord appeared and said, *"The Lord is with you, thou mighty man of valor"* (Judges 6:12).

Although Gideon was in a cowardly position, God saw him as a champion and warrior. God does not see us for who we are but for who we can be in Him. Gideon responds to the angel in disbelief. Gideon began to explain to God the predicament that Israel was in as though God was in the dark on the events that had taken place.

> Judges 6:13-16: *"If the Lord be with us, why then is all this befallen us? And where be all his miracles which our fathers told us of, saying, Did not the Lord bring us up from Egypt? But now the Lord hath*

forsaken us and delivered us into the hands of the Midianites. And the Lord looked upon him and said, Go in this thy might, and thou shalt save Israel from the hand of the Midianites: have not I sent thee? And he said unto him, Oh my Lord, wherewith shall I save Israel? Behold, my family is poor in Manasseh, and I am the least in my father's house. And the Lord said unto him, Surely I will be with thee, and thou shalt smite the Midianites as one man."

Despite all of Gideon's excuses, God saw something in him that he could not see in himself. Possibility and potential may have appeared to be dormant, but they were present. All things are possible with God. Gideon had to fight through fear, feelings of being forsaken, and the fear of being incapable of doing the job. But God reassured him that He was with him.

God calls Gideon from a place of complacency and contentment. When God's hands are on your life, prolonged mediocrity is not sustainable. Too often, we allow ourselves to be intimidated by the enormity of the circumstances that we face. As a result, we become immobilized and paralyzed by our fears.

Next, God speaks into the weaknesses of Gideon and pulls courage out of him. God does this by first assuring him that He is with him; If Gideon had no reason to take courage before this moment, he now had a reason. Gideon reflected on God's track record— how the hand of God had worked on behalf of Israel before bringing them out of Egypt, across the Red Sea, and into the Promised Land. It was proof that God could do what He said He would do.

Courage is what this generation needs to navigate the unique challenges of today. This generation is presented with issues that generations in the past never had to face. Challenges include the mainstreaming of the occult, the new age movement, and false doctrine that is even more subtle in its recruitment and seduction; sexual perversion is presented as a usual way of life. Drugs and other addictive practices are becoming more readily available to children and young people at earlier ages. There is a spiritual battle raging in this generation.

Ephesians 6:12: "*For we wrestle not against flesh and blood, but against principalities, against powers, against the rulers of the darkness of this world, against spiritual wickedness in high places.*"

Gideon's character was also revealed through this test. Notice how Gideon first points back to his heritage. Gideon said to God, "*I am from the tribe of Manasseh, one of the smallest tribes of among the children of Israel. I am the least in my father's house.*"

By saying this, Gideon revealed his humility. It is not the proud and the "most likely to succeed" that God chooses to use, but those who will humble themselves and become pliable in His hands. Gideon was able to move past his sense of inadequacy and low self-esteem. He led an army of 300 young men to victory in a battle that could not be naturally won. He did so because of courage and character.

God had to reassure Gideon that he was capable of taking on this challenge. It was not enough for Gideon to hear the words, *"Thou mighty man of valor,"* but God also tells him, *"Go in this thy might, and thou shalt save Israel from the hand of the Midianites: have not I sent you."*

Gideon, God has prepared you for this feat. In other words, you can accomplish what may seem impossible.

I speak the same life into this generation and reassure them that the God Who has called them has already equipped them to overcome the giants before them. You will possess the gates of your enemies. You will inherit the land that God has promised you. You shall walk into doors that were once locked to your ancestors. You will be CEOs of Fortune 500 corporations. You will occupy political offices that were not available to your family before you. You will be all that God has ordained you to be. Walk boldly in the understanding that God has called you to the kingdom for such a time like this. You are God's righteous seed to this generation.

Zechariah 4:6: *"It is not by might nor by power but by God's spirit saith the Lord."*

Finally, Gideon had to be given the confidence that he was a conqueror. God dwindles Gideon's army down by 29,000 to further solidify that the victory would be through Him—not by physical strength. There must have been some nervousness that crept into Gideon's thoughts. However, with an army of only 300 men, Gideon defeated an army of more than 300,000 Midianites.

"What shall we say to these things? If God be for us, who can be against us?" (Romans 8:31).

God delivered Gideon just as He said He would. He caused Gideon to defeat the armies of the Midianites. As God was with Gideon, so is God going to be with you as you tackle the adversities that stand before you.

> Romans 8:37: *"Nay, in all these things we are more than conquerors through him that loved us."*

The story of Gideon's victories did not end there. The Bible tells of two kings of Midian who escaped the battle to a place called Succoth. Gideon and his men apprehended them (Judges 8:12). Gideon asked the kings, Zebah and Zelmunna, *"Who were the men you killed at Tabor?"* (Judges 8:18).

The importance of this encounter is revealed in the definition of these names presented in the passage. The name Tabor means "pinnacle or height." Tabor was the place where young men of Israel were slain, a high place. The name Zebah means "sacrifice" (Strong, 1890). Perhaps these boys were killed as a sacrifice offered to their god. The enemy desires to kill our young people before they can walk in the fullness of their purpose and before they ever have the opportunity to accomplish the great things that God has in store for them.

Zelmunna means "shade has been denied" (Strong, 1890). This implies that there was no protection. Our parental guidance and our prayers cover our children. Even so, there are places that the shade of our prayers does not extend, places where they find themselves exposed and vulnerable to Satan's attacks.

It is what happened to the men that Gideon was inquiring about. The response that Zebah and Zelmunna give shines even more light on the situation:

Judges 8:18b says, *"And they answered, As thou art, so were they; each one resembled the children of a king."*

Those words were both revealing and tragic at the same time. The young men had the appearance of greatness, but the young men were cut off from ever reaching their full potential.

"Gideon as thou art, so are they" (Judges 8:18). Young men with the same capability, courage, and spirit of a conqueror; were silenced in death without an opportunity to reach their potential.

How many sons and daughters must endure the same end? These young men represented righteous seed on the earth. Men poised to take positions of eldership in Israel. Satan would love to have this be the epitaph of this generation. How many children have been killed by drive-by shootings, by the people sworn to protect, by suicide, and by abortions?

There is much debate in religious circles, political parties, and barbershop conversations on whether abortions are right or wrong. Statistics do not lie. Year after year, children that could have been righteous seeds to declare the wisdom of God are aborted. This chapter is not about a political argument concerning abortion, but I must stand up for the right of babies whose voices will never be heard. These innocent babies had no choice in their outcome.

"Roe v. Wade, 410 U.S. 113 (1973), [1] was a landmark decision of the U.S. Supreme Court in which the Court ruled that the Constitution of the United States protects a pregnant woman's liberty to choose to have an abortion without excessive government restriction. It struck down many U.S. federal and state abortion laws, [2][3] and prompted an ongoing national debate in the United States about whether and to what extent abortion should be legal, who should decide the legality of abortion, what methods the Supreme Court should use in constitutional adjudication, and what the role of religious and moral views in the political sphere should be. Roe v. Wade reshaped American politics, dividing much of the United States into abortion rights and anti-abortion movements, while activating grassroots movements on both sides" (Levine, 1999).

"The decision involved the case of a woman named Norma McCorvey—known in her lawsuit under the pseudonym "Jane Roe"—who in 1969 became pregnant with her third child. McCorvey wanted an abortion, but she lived in Texas, where abortion was illegal except when necessary, to save the mother's life. She was referred to lawyers Sarah Weddington and Linda Coffee, who filed a lawsuit on her behalf in U.S. federal court against her local district attorney, Henry Wade, alleging that Texas's abortion laws were unconstitutional. A three-judge panel of the U.S. District Court for the Northern District of Texas heard the case and ruled in her favor. Texas then appealed this ruling directly to the U.S. Supreme Court, which agreed to hear the case" (Levine, 1999).

"In January 1973, the Supreme Court issued a 7–2 decision ruling that the Due Process Clause of the Fourteenth Amendment to the U.S. Constitution provides a "right to privacy" that protects a pregnant woman's right to choose whether or not to have an abortion. But it also ruled that this right is not absolute, and must be balanced against the government's interests in protecting women's health and protecting prenatal life.[4][5] The Court resolved this balancing test by tying state regulation of abortion to the three trimesters of pregnancy: during the first trimester, governments could not prohibit abortions at all; during the second trimester, governments could require reasonable health regulations; during the third trimester, abortions could be prohibited entirely so long as the laws contained exceptions for cases when they were necessary to save the life or health of the mother.[5] The Court classified the right to choose to have an abortion as "fundamental", which required courts to evaluate challenged abortion laws under the "strict scrutiny" standard, the highest level of judicial review in the United States"[6] (Levine, 1999).

The number of abortions has increased steadily and dramatically since 1970. These statistics span from 1970-2016.

Year Number of abortions reported to CDC Number of abortions per 1,000 women aged 15–44 years (Rate) Number of abortions per 1,000 live births (Ratio) CDC Abortion Surveillance Report

1970	193,491	5	52	[5]
1971	485,816	11	137	[5]
1972	586,760	13	180	[5]

1973	615,831	14	196	[5]
1974	763,476	17	242	[5]
1975	854,853	18	272	[5]
1976	988,267	21	312	[5]
1977	950,675	22	325	[5]
1978	1,157,776	23	347	[5]
1979	1,251,921	24	358	[7]
1980	1,297,606	25	359	[7]
1981	1,300,760	24	358	[8]
1982	1,303,980	24	354	[5]
1983	1,268,987	23	349	[5]
1984	1,333,521	24	364	[9]
1985	1,328,570	24	354	[9]
1986	1,328,112	23	354	[10]
1987	1,353,671	24	356	[10]
1988	1,371,285	24	352	[11]
1989	1,396,658	24	346	[12]
1990	1,429,247	24	345	[13]

1991	1,388,937	24	339	[14]
1992	1,359,145	23	335	[15]
1993	1,330,414	23	334	[16]
1994	1,267,415	21	321	[16]
1995	1,210,883	20	311	[17]
1996	1,221,585	21	314	[18]
1997	1,186,039	20	274	[19]
1998	884,273	17	264	[20]
1999	861,789	17	256	[21]
2000	857,475	16	246	[22]
2001	853,485	16	246	[23]
2002	854,122	16	246	[24]
2003	848,163	16	241	[25]
2004	839,226	16	238	[26]
2005	820,151	15	233	[5]
2006	846,181	15.9	236	[27]
2007	827,609	15.6	231	[28]
2008	825,564	15.6	234	[29]

2009	789,507	14.9	227	[30]
2010	765,651	14.4	228	[31]
2011	730,322	13.7	219	[32]
2012	699,202	13.1	210	[33]
2013	664,435	12.4	200	[34]
2014	652,639	12.1	186	[35]
2015	638,169	11.8	188	[6]
2016	623,471	11.6	186	[4]

These statistics reveal a total number of 60,000,000 abortions between 1970 and 2016; 60,000,000 souls who could have made world-changing contributions to our world.

> Jeremiah 31:15-17: *"Thus saith the Lord; A voice was heard in Ramah, lamentation, and bitter weeping; Rachel weeping for her children refused to be comforted for her children, because they were not. Thus saith the Lord; Refrain thy voice from weeping, and thine eyes from tears: for thy work shall be rewarded, saith the Lord; and they shall come again from the land of the enemy. And there is hope in thine end, saith the Lord, that thy children shall come again to their own border."*

The writer paints a picture of Rachel, the mother of Benjamin and Joseph, weeping over her children. Rachel is crying from the place where she was buried, Ramah, weeping from the tomb because the children of Israel had been taken captive and placed in exile.

There is an alarm being sounded in this hour, waking up our spiritual leaders to problems that presently grip our society. Where are the spiritual parents who are crying out for this generation that finds themselves at a crossroad? This generation has the opportunity to take on the mantle of righteousness, or they can choose to reject the call of God and go after other gods.

The Bible said that Rachel refused to be comforted as long as her children were not at rest. There was a promise that the children of Israel would come back from the land of the enemy, indicating to His people that there is hope for the future. No matter how much pain and tribulation the time of exile might bring, it would not be their final chapter. Who will be the spiritual 'Rachels' of our time prepared to give birth to the righteous seed that will usher in God's wave in the last days?

This same imagery was also used in the Book of Matthew when Herod sought to kill all of the male children two years and younger to avoid the prophecy of the King's birth (Matthew 2:16-18). Just as The divine purpose of God nullified Herod's plan, I believe there will be those who will rise up from this generation and fulfill God's divine purpose for this time.

God told Jeremiah, *"Before I formed you in the belly, I knew you: and before thou camest forth out of the womb I sanctified you, and I ordained you a prophet unto the nations"* (Jeremiah 1:5).

Despite the spirit of intimidation and low self-esteem that wants to seize this generation, that which God spoke over their lives while they were being formed in the womb shall come forth. The *'Joshuas'* and the *'Esthers'* will seize the moment and tackle the giants of our day with the anointing and wisdom of God. Rachel will rise from her weeping, and she shall shout with praise as the righteous seed stands up in victory. Her children would come back from the land of the enemy. God's promise of restoration means there is hope, even for future generations.

Why is this subject so dear to me? I can remember the excitement my wife and I had when the doctors told us that she was pregnant with our first child. We could not wait to tell family members our good news. Just months later, the doctor told us there was a possibility they would have to perform an abortion because the baby was lodged in the fallopian tube. The doctor said if they did not do an abortion, the tube could burst, and my wife could die as a result.

We had only been married for two years, and now we're confronted with the hardest decision of our lives. We knew what we saw when the doctors showed us the ultrasound, which confirmed what he had told us. We decided to go home and pray about the decision that we would make. After two weeks of prayer, we went back to the doctor, and suddenly there was a change in the egg's position in the tube. The egg would come to be known later as our oldest child, Ashley Lydia Lauren Ramsey, who was born healthy and without any ill effects of any kind.

What if this beautiful, creative, and anointed woman of God had been prematurely aborted? Ashley would have never had the opportunity to preach on some of the largest platforms in her denomination. She would have never written books, started a Giant Slayers conference, and been a trailblazer in this generation. Yet, some children will never have that opportunity because of premature deaths for all kinds of reasons.

Some young people are ready to be released into their destiny. No matter how much negative information has been disseminated about the youth of this generation, I still believe there is a righteous seed that is waiting in the shadows. My daughter's story is the same story for many other young people who have the potential and the ability to do great things. But they are waiting on spiritual fathers and mothers to take them under their wings and pray them into their destiny and purpose. Spiritual parents have a responsibility to protect and preserve the spiritual seed of the present and beyond.

> Psalm 112:1-2: *"Praise ye the Lord. Blessed is the man that feareth the Lord, that delighteth greatly in his commandments. His seed shall be mighty upon earth: the generation of the upright shall be blessed."*

Chapter 8

Absence of Servant Leadership

It was a hot sunny morning in Miami, Florida, when my pastor, Bishop Walter D. Jackson, asked several young men to meet him at the church. What seemed to be an impromptu meeting at church would be a life lesson that I would never forget. The reason for the gathering turned out to be to assist him in cleaning up the perimeter of the church. I distinctly remember pulling up the weeds and aloe plants that cluttered the outside of the church. The bushes had been there for months, but on that day, our efforts transformed the curb appeal of our beloved home church.

What about that was life-altering? From experience, I learned firsthand that leading a ministry extended beyond standing behind a pulpit every Sunday. Leadership is not just glitz and glamour. Sometimes you have to give sweat and labor *if* you are going to bring about change. Bishop Jackson was not a young man, but he was not outworked by any young men who labored with him that day.

Bishop Jackson did not just issue a directive, but he demonstrated what it meant to be sacrificial and unselfish in ministry. Seeing him at work gave me a different perspective of him as a pastor and as a leader. It was authentic servant leadership on display. Two of the young men who Bishop Jackson chose to work with that day became pastors of local churches, and the other two became dedicated laymen at their local church. These are the kind of opportunities that prepared us for the call to serve.

In observing today's leaders, it appears that many have failed to recognize the kind of example Bishop Jackson set. It is as if ministers have moved away from this ministry model—ministers of today have greatly forsaken the ministry of sacrifice.

Matthew 20:28 says, "*Just as the Son of Man did not come to be served, but to serve, and to give His life a ransom for many.*"

The example that my former pastor set for us demonstrated the highest level of ministry, servanthood.

In no way am I saying that ministers should be disregarded and disrespected. Still, a level of humility must correspond with the level of honor and respect afforded to us as ministers. Pride and arrogance have no place in the kingdom of God and even more so in the life of a representative of the Lord Jesus Christ.

Proverbs 16:18: *"Pride goeth before destruction, and a haughty spirit before a fall."*

Proverbs 11:2: *"When pride cometh, then cometh shame: but with the lowly is wisdom."*

The media takes pleasure in spotlighting ministers who live extravagant lives while most people in their congregations live below poverty income lines. Some ministers have humble beginnings, but they amass success and notoriety through hard work, dedication, and zeal. Because their social elevation often feels sudden, they're usually not experienced enough to handle the seemingly overnight success. Then some are inexperienced ministers unwilling to serve under those who are more established in the ministry to build the necessary experience to be successful.

In 1 Timothy 3:1-7, Paul gives a young Timothy instruction on how to identify the appropriate ministers for the office of the bishop. Speaking of such ministers, the scriptures say that *"He must be above reproach, the husband of one wife, temperate or have a spirit of self-control, prudent, respectable, hospitable, able to teach, not addicted to wine or pugnacious, but gentle, peaceable, free from the love of money. He must be one who manages his own household well, keep his children under control with all dignity. But if a man does not know how to manage his own household, how will he take care of the church of God, and not a new convert, so that he will not become conceited and fall into the condemnation incurred by the devil."*

I want to specifically look at the term new convert or newcomer, synonymous with *novice, beginner, learner, or neophyte.* In the King James Version, the word novice derives from the Greek word (neuphotos), literally meaning 'newly planted.' Paul saw a danger in elevating men and women of God who had not been properly trained and developed into high positions of oversight too quickly (Guzik, 2018).

Calvin commented that *"Novices are not only bold and impetuous, but are puffed up with foolish self-confidence, as though they could fly beyond the clouds"* (Guzik, 2018: 1 Timothy 3, Qualifications for Leaders,).

These guidelines were given to protect the person desiring the office and the people they would oversee.

As a young pastor, I felt slighted that I held degrees that many men appointed as Bishops over me did not possess. I did not fully understand this being a young man just out of seminary. Like most young ministers, I felt I had the training necessary to do the job of an overseer. What I did not understand at the time was that some knowledge could not be gained from a book or in a classroom setting. Some qualifying knowledge only comes through firsthand experiences and real-time challenges in ministry.

The amount of time I had spent and learned from older and more experienced ministers gave me an advantage over some of my contemporaries who were also coming out of college and seminary. However, that was still not enough to prevent me from experiencing the same pitfalls Paul was addressing. You can mean well and at the same time be overly ambitious, full of pride and arrogance, and because of inexperience, even fall into the traps of sin. Looking back over my life, I can truly say it was nothing but the grace of God that has kept me.

Years ago, there was an unspoken policy that church leaders implemented; they would start the new minister out in a small church, allowing the minister to get his feet wet. Based on the minister's aptitude and commitment, he would then be promoted to a larger congregation. But only after he attained a level of competence revealed he was ready to handle the larger congregations in the denomination. I am a product of this process, and in retrospect, I understand it clearly.

Today, I can see where there is still a need for an training process in pastoral development. I have seen many ministers who have attempted to circumvent this process find themselves in situations they were too underdeveloped to manage. They were faced with challenges and ministry demands they were too inexperienced to meet.

On one occasion, I distinctly remember when I was appointed to a church. My District Overseer stood out in the parking lot talking to the state overseer, and he said, "*This church is going to make him or break him.*" He was right; that church helped mold me into the minister I am today.

I look back over my life with renewed gratitude to God for the ministers and mentors He placed around me who aided in my growth and maturation and helped guide me toward the proper paths.

Within my denomination, some guidelines and requirements must be met to reach the rank of Ordained Bishop. There came a time in my life where I felt that I had met those qualifications. Although I was set forth by the local church as prescribed by those guidelines, my District Bishop thought that I needed to wait four more years. As a result, he did not sign off on my application. I was distraught and bewildered by my District Bishop's decision. I did not understand at the time that it was all in God's plan. At the time, I had been in ministry for eight years and had never faced such an obstacle. After over 40 years of ministry, I know that *obstacle* was merely a drop in the bucket compared to what I would encounter in this ministerial journey. I thank God for that district overseer, and if he were alive today, I would honor him for his wisdom and foresight.

The wise bishops of old understood a principle that Paul was attempting to teach a young Timothy. Today, we need more spiritual fathers who will speak the truth even when it is not well received, set boundaries, and help newcomers avoid the traps the devil has placed in the shadows.

I must tell you this story does not end here. I also want to thank God for the Bishop who was over the examining board, who came to me and said, *"I understand what happened four years ago, and I see the hand of God on your life, and I want to recommend you for the office of Bishop personally."* In that Bishop's latter years, I became the Regional Bishop who had supervisory responsibilities over him. He shared with me at the time that he was proud to serve under my leadership.

The call of Elisha displays this principle. Elijah, the elder prophet, had just been commissioned by God to anoint Hazael king over Aram and Jehu, the son of Nimshi, King over Israel. The Bible says Elijah departed from there and found Elisha. It was almost as if by the divine leading of the Holy Spirit that Elijah connected to Elisha. It was not a coincidence or by accident. God had a plan for Elisha's life, and it required an impartation from a person who fully understood the magnitude of the call (1 Kings 19:15-19).

The Bible tells us to lay hands on no man suddenly (1 Timothy 5:22). We need men and women of God who will have their ear to God's mouth and discern the divine calling on the lives of those they are called to oversee. I thank God for the missionaries and ministers who spoke into my life down through the years, imparting both wisdom and truth at critical intervals of my Christian experience. It was the impact that Elijah had on the life of Elisha.

There was something about Elijah that caught the attention of Elisha to the extent that he was willing to leave everything to follow Elijah.

Matthew 16:24 says: *"Then said Jesus unto his disciples, If any man will come after me, let him deny himself, and take up his cross, and follow me."*

Although these words were spoken after Elisha's time, Elisha's actions exemplified this verse correctly. Elisha took immediate steps which shifted the course of his life forever. Elisha went from being a full-time farmer to being a full-time prophet of God.

It is important to note that Elisha did not go away and take time to think about what was happening. Elisha did not make up a list of pros and cons about what life decision he should make next, nor did Elisha choose to play it safe. It was almost as if Elisha gave an immediately answered *'yes'* to the call. Elisha's commitment was complete, insomuch that he was willing to leave everything that he loved dearly. Sometimes the step toward your destiny is a step away from all that you know and all that provides you strength and security.

Elisha had to be willing to leave the familiar for the unfamiliar because the moment he accepted the call, it would be expected that some separation would occur. Elisha's life was going to be dramatically different. The assignment he was being called to would require him to separate from his father and his mother, separate from his friends, and separate from the place he called home. All of these relationships were going to have to be abandoned for Elisha to follow Elijah. Even with the enormity of the decision, nothing appeared to discourage Elisha from the choice he was making.

Elisha disconnected himself from everything he had come to know as part of his identity and heritage. In disconnecting himself from the familiar, he was making a divine connection of unlimited potential. When we branch out into new vineyards, there is always a risk associated with our choice to venture out. For Elisha, the perceived benefits were far greater than the fear of any losses.

Elisha said to Elijah, "*Let me kiss my father and my mother, and then I will follow thee*" (1 Kings 19:20). Can you imagine what those final moments Elisha had with his parents must have been like? Maybe you can visualize his mother with tears streaming down her eyes, consumed by the thought of her son leaving. Imagine his father grappling with the thought of his legacy—his son departs. Elisha's parents may have been growing older. This may have been when most children were expected to be the family's future's primary security. In this season of their life, Elisha was departing. A final kiss, a final goodbye, a powerful moment that immediately propelled Elisha into an unfamiliar world.

I have heard many missionaries share their stories. Many of them speak of the adjustments they had to make, the new relationships they had to establish, and the pain that came with being far away from the life they once knew. Separation is never easy, but Jesus comforted us by saying, *"And every one that hath forsaken houses, or brethren, or sister, or father, or mother, or wife, or children, or lands, for my name's sake, shall receive a hundredfold, and shall inherit everlasting life"* (Matthew 19:29).

There have been two times in my life when I had to pack up and leave a community that had grown so familiar to me. I learned the blessing of trusting God's plan on both occasions, even when it did not make sense.

Not only did Elisha's choice require separation, but it also would call for him to live a life of servitude. Elisha would serve Elijah. We have the picture of Elijah throwing his mantle on Elisha. It communicates the clear message that before we can wear the mantle of anointing needed for ministry, we must be willing to wear the mantle of servitude.

Some commentators say that Elisha washed the feet of Elijah.

He was Elijah's attendant. But while he was in servitude to Elijah, he was also a prophet in training. His service was a part of his training. Think about it, washing someone's feet. In those days, many times, the journey was with bare feet. The roads were dirty and filled with rocks. Most people do not want the responsibility of washing their own feet, but Elisha was called to the ministry of washing feet.

Jesus used the washing of feet to teach the disciples the true meaning of servanthood:

> John 13:12-17: *"So after he had washed their feet, and had taken his garments, and was set down again, he said unto them, Know ye what I have done to you? Ye call me Master and Lord: and ye say well; for so I am. If I then, your Lord and Master, have washed your feet; ye also ought to wash one another's feet. For I have given you an example, that ye should do as I have done to you. Verily, verily, I say unto you, The servant is not greater than his lord; neither he that is sent greater than he that sent him. If ye know these things, happy are ye if ye do them."*

Peter questioned the act of Jesus washing the disciple's feet, but Jesus responded, *"If I wash thee not, thou hast no part with me"* (John 13:8). Peter immediately becomes repentant and asks Jesus to wash his feet and his hands and head.

Washing his master's feet was an opportunity Elisha took to be connected to Elijah. Elisha's actions of washing his master's feet is a model for each of us to look to as we pattern ourselves after the example of Jesus Christ.

In 2 Kings 3:11, Elisha is identified by his service to Elijah—*"And one of the king of Israel's servants answered and said, Here is Elisha the son of Shaphat, which poured water on the hands of Elijah."* Elisha's service to Elijah caused him to stand out. The question is, how do people identify us when it comes to ministry?

Finally, Elisha's decision to follow Elijah came with him making the supreme sacrifice. Elisha is seen initially plowing with a yoke of oxen. To have 12 yokes of oxen, Elisha's parents must have had a vast field to plow, meaning that Elisha's parents were possibly very wealthy. Even with this assumed wealth, it was costly for Elisha to take a yoke of oxen, slay them, and then give them to the people in the community to eat (1 Kings 19:21). But Elisha was so committed to the call that he would be willing to give up all.

This act was the sacrifice of his livelihood, his future, and his parent's security. It took a step of faith. How was Elisha going to survive? What was going to be the future for his parents? Without these answers, Elisha still killed the oxen and fed them to the people.

Ministry continually comes with great sacrifices, even without having all the answers. Napoleon Hill said, *"Great achievement is usually born of great sacrifice, and is never the result of selfishness"* (Hill, n.d.). Sacrifice requires going beyond your ambitions and hopes for the future. One definition of sacrifice is surrendering a possession as an offering to God or a divine or supernatural figure. It is what Elisha did. He sacrificed his wealth, stability, and comforts.

Sometimes suffering comes with sacrifice, but with much sacrifice, God is well pleased. The reality is that anytime we make a sacrifice for the cause of Christ, it is never a sacrifice without God's promise.

All through Scripture, people of faith have made sacrifices. Jesus told the disciples to follow Him, and He would make them fishers of men. God told Abraham to go up to Mount Moriah and offer up his only son. Esther was willing to sacrifice her life to save her people from the gallows of Haman. Jesus made the ultimate sacrifice by going to the cross and offering up His life as a ransom for our sins.

Paul said in Philippians 3:8, "*Yea doubtless, and I count all things but loss for the excellency of the knowledge of Christ Jesus my Lord, for whom I have suffered the loss of all things and count them but dung, that I may win Christ.*"

Like Paul, Elisha saw ministry as his primary focus. No price was too high to pay; no sacrifice was too steep for the cause of the ministry. Ministers today must also be willing to make sacrifices that may be initially challenging but will perpetually pay dividends in the long run.

Elisha receiving a double portion of Elijah's anointing was worth the time of separation. It was worth the times of servitude, and it was worth all that he sacrificed. All of these acts of servitude are the very things that catapulted him into a ministry that saw dead bodies raised, saw God do amazing miracles and the appearance of angelic reinforcements in his time of need.

The question is often asked, *how do you measure success?* Elisha did twice as many miracles as Elijah. Even after Elisha's death, his bones still carried enough anointing to raise a dead man after being thrown in Elisha's tomb. If I were able to ask Elisha any question, I'd ask, *what were some of the things that prepared you for the ministry that was ahead of you?* In my estimation, it would undoubtedly be the act of separation, the act of servanthood, and the willingness to make selfless sacrifices. Servanthood is what I consider to be the highest measure of success. Elisha had the spirit of a servant.

Chapter 9

Absence of Honor and Respect

Principles that were lost over the years are honor and respect, especially for those who are elderly. I remember my grandmother, Mother Georgiana Ramsey, stressing the importance of respecting their elders to her grandchildren. She would insist that we respond by saying, *"yes, ma'am or yes, sir," "thank you, sir,"* and *"thank you, ma'am."* These words were a part of our everyday speech. We were never allowed to call our elders by their first names. If you happened to slip and say or do something inappropriate by chance, you were verbally reprimanded in public and could also expect some corporal punishment. I do not consider the discipline I received as a child as demoralizing or as an act of breaking my spirit. It was a way of deterring me from unnecessary hardships and tears that could come later in life. Proverbs 22:15 says, "*Foolishness is bound in the heart of a child; but the rod of correction shall drive it far from him.*" Unmistakably, this scripture has proven to be true in my lifetime.

Today, it is common for children to disrespect their parents publicly. It has gotten to the point where even some parents are now afraid of their children! I have seen young children having temper tantrums in the grocery store or in a mall. The children fall all on the ground to get their way. Then the parent, rather than deal with the child's behavior, gives the child the toy or candy to appease and silence them.

A friend of mine recently sent me a video that demonstrates this very dynamic. The video is of an infant who was about six months old. The infant had developed an affinity for a particular cellphone. As long as the baby held the phone in its hands, the baby was quiet and well-mannered. The moment the phone was taken away, the baby rolled over and cried profusely until the phone was again presented to him. Once the baby held the phone in his hand, he immediately became as quiet as a lamb.

Although the video initially appeared to be hilarious, in reality, it reveals a serious issue in today's society. This type of response to inappropriate behavior has contributed to the loss of parental control and discipline. The loss of discipline follows the decline of honor and respect for those responsible for our care and protection.

Ephesians 6:1-3 says, *"Children, obey your parents in the Lord: for this is right. Honor thy father and mother; which is the first commandment with promise; That it may be well with thee, and thou mayest live long on the earth."*

In my life, God has opened many avenues and opportunities to travel all over the world. In my travels, I have been exposed to and have observed many cultures. In my trips to the region of West Africa, I have observed how honor and respect are demonstrated. Men and women who serve alongside leaders exhibit a great sense of loyalty and high regard for those they serve under in ministry. Many men and women call their leaders *father* and *mother* as a term of endearment and a display of honor. Whatever they were tasked to do was done wholeheartedly and in reverence to their leader. In coming back to the United States, I noticed a distinct difference in how we engage with our leaders, and it has left me a little disheartened.

In America, there is the overwhelming sentiment that respect and honor must be earned. Though this is accurate, the danger in this philosophy is that it is often rooted in the place of disregard for established and ordained leadership. Unfortunately, some examples of spiritual fathers have manipulated and taken advantage of those who serve under them. There have been cases of spiritual fathers using and discarding people when they no longer serve their purpose. Therefore, understanding on both sides of the spectrum should happen to have mutual respect and honor. God has commissioned us to have respect for those who have the rule over us in Him. When spiritual fathers fail their God-given charge to be a covering, we must pray for them and leave them in the hands of the Lord.

I believe the loss of honor and respect for spiritual leadership is directly correlated with the loss of honor and respect for God and His Word in modern society. There was a time where those who grew up in the Church were expected to abstain from certain activities and scenarios. However, questionable and compromising situations have become commonplace in the family of God. There is a growing loss of reverence for God.

Proverbs 9:10 says, *"The fear of the Lord is the beginning of wisdom: and the knowledge of the holy is understanding."*

Scripture teaches us that wisdom is acknowledging the greatness, holiness, and transcending power of God.

God is SOVEREIGN

God's Sovereignty - God rules over all; He is Lord; He is God. El Shaddai, the Lord God Almighty. El Elyon, the Most-High God.

1 Chronicles 29:11-12: *"Thine, O Lord is the greatness, and the power, and the glory, and the victory, and the majesty: for all that is in the heaven and in the earth is thine; thine is the kingdom, O Lord, and thou art exalted as head above all. Both riches and honor come of thee, and thou reignest over all; and in thine hand is power and might; and in thine hand it is to make great, and to give strength unto all."*

Psalm 103:19: *"The Lord hath prepared his throne in the heavens; and his kingdom ruleth overall."*

Psalm 115:3: *"But our God is in the heavens: he hath done whatsoever he hath pleased."*

Psalm 147:5: *"Great is our Lord, and of great power: his understanding is infinite."*

TRANSCENDENCY OF GOD

God is transcendent-above all, beyond all; He is supreme, preeminent, superior, unsurpassed, incomparable. Yet the God who is so great and mighty stoops down to man to have a relationship with him.

> Isaiah 55:8-9: *"For my thoughts are not your thoughts, neither are your ways my ways, saith the Lord. For as the heavens are higher than the earth, so are my ways higher than your ways, and my thoughts than your thoughts."*

> Isaiah 40:22: *"It is he that sitteth upon the circle of the earth, and the inhabitants thereof are as grasshoppers; that stretcheth out the heavens as a curtain, and spreadeth them out as a tent to dwell in."*

> Psalm 97:9: *"For thou, Lord, art high above all the earth: thou art exalted far above all."*

> Hebrews 1:3: *"Who being the brightness of his glory, and the express image of his person, and upholding all things by the word of his power, when he had by himself purged our sins, sat down on the right hand of the Majesty on high."*

> Acts 7:49: *"Heaven is my throne, and earth is my footstool: what house will ye build me? saith the Lord: or what is the place of my rest?"*

God is HOLY

Not only is God sovereign and transcendent, but He is holy and righteous. God is perfect purity, perfect truth, perfect righteousness.

> 1 Samuel 2:2: *"There is none holy as the Lord: for there is none beside thee: neither is there any rock like our God."*

Isaiah 6:3: *"And one cried unto another, and said, Holy, holy, holy, is the Lord of hosts: the whole earth is full of his glory."*

Leviticus 19:2: *"Speak unto all the congregation of the children of Israel, and say unto them, Ye shall be holy: for I the Lord your God am holy."*

Isaiah 57:15: *"For thus saith the high and lofty One that inhabiteth eternity, whose name is Holy; I dwell in the high and holy place, with him also that is of a contrite and humble spirit, to revive the spirit of the humble, and to revive the heart of the contrite ones."*

God is so pure, matchless, and unique; He is incomparable. He is altogether glorious—unequaled in splendor and unrivaled in power. He is beyond the grasp of human reason—far above the reach of even the loftiest scientific mind. He is inexhaustible, immeasurable, and unfathomable—eternal, immortal, and invisible. The highest mountain peaks and the deepest canyon depths do not even amount to tiny echoes of His proclaimed greatness. The blazing stars above are merely the faintest emblems of the full measure of His glory.

Israel often experienced the greatness of God in the miracles He performed during their deliverance out of Egypt by their God-ordained leader, Moses. They saw how God used ten plagues to bring Pharoah to his knees. In addition, they saw how God opened up the Red Sea and caused the children of Israel to walk across on dry ground. God used the same Red Sea to swallow the armies of

Pharaoh that had pursued the children of Israel (Exodus 14). Yet, in all the wonders God performed before their eyes, they still turned their backs on God and their leader, Moses. We can see a correlation between the days of Moses and the present times.

In Moses' day, Israel lost honor and respect for the sacredness of God. The loss of reverence for God trickled down to the loss of respect for the leadership He ordained to lead the people.

When we speak of the Holiness of God, it reminds us of how unworthy we are of His mercy and His grace. It is awe-inspiring how God keeps on loving us despite our faults and our failures. Israel may have repeatedly failed God, but God consistently never failed them. God continued to be a Father and raise spiritual fathers to guide them—an infinite God in relationship with a finite man.

> Psalm 8:3-4*: "When I consider thy heavens, the work of thy fingers, the moon and the stars, which thou hast ordained; What is man, that thou art mindful of him? and the son of man, that thou visitest him?"*

Amazingly, an awesome all-powerful God would descend to lowly man and have fellowship with him. A holy and righteous God, calling fallen sinful mankind into right relationship with Himself through spiritual fathers. When we take into consideration God's greatness, it should provoke reverence and honor toward Him. If men of God today can find themselves submitted to the will and purposes of this holy God, the people they serve can again see them in a place of honor and respect. This alone can be a big step toward spiritual fathers regaining the honor and respect that has been lost over time.

In an article by Moneywise on November 20, 2019, Scott Nordlund ranked professions from most to least respected. Of that list, Clergy was seventeenth on the list (Nordlund, 2019).

27. Nurses (Most respected)

26. Military officers

25. Medical Doctors

24. Grade School Teachers

23. Engineers

22. Pharmacists

21. Dentists

20. Day Care Providers

19. Police Officers

18. Psychiatrists

17. Clergyman

16. Chiropractors

15. Auto mechanics

14. Judges

13. College Teachers

12. Local Officeholders

11. Bankers

10. Nursing Home Operators

9. Lawyers

8. Business Executives

7. State Office Holders

6. Advertising Professionals

5. Newspapers Reporters

4. Television Reporters

3. Car Salesperson

2. Lobbyists

1. Members of Congress (Least Respected)

There was a time when clergymen were the first source of support people would contact in crisis moments or for counseling, but that trend has dramatically declined. *"Historians say public attitudes about clergy have been waning since the 1970s, in tandem with the loss of trust in institutions after the Vietnam War and the Watergate scandal"* (Shimron, 2019).

Seventy-Five percent of churchgoers hold clergy in very high regard, although they are not as positive regarding their clergy's attributes and character qualities. It is said that half of the churchgoers consider clergy to be trustworthy, and only slightly more recognize them as honest and intelligent (Stonestreet & Rivera, 2019). The startling truth is that in past decades clergy were seen as one of the most respected professions. Over time, there has been a decline in respect due to the moral failures of popular televangelists and the growing distrust of institutions as a whole.

Therefore, there is an understanding of why people behave the way they do toward leaders with a sense of skepticism and hesitation. However, we must understand that despite what our personal experiences may have been in the past, we are commanded by the Word of God to respect those who have the rule over us in the Lord.

> Hebrews 13:17: *"Obey them that have the rule over you and submit yourselves: for they watch for your souls, as they that must give account, that they may do it with joy, and not with grief: for that is unprofitable for you."*

> Colossians 3:20: *"Children, obey your parents in all things: for this is well pleasing unto the Lord."*

The Bible speaks explicitly about the importance of honor and respect for those in leadership and the parents God has given us. In Paul's letter to the Ephesians and the Colossian saints, he instructs children to obey their parents. His letter to the Ephesians goes even further by stating that you must be obedient to your parents for your life to be extended. The Fifth commandment was given to Moses on Mount Sinai also connects the length of life with obedience to parents:

Exodus 20:12 *"Honor thy father and mother, that thy days may be long upon the land which the Lord they God giveth thee."*

We can see here the law of repetition. The law of repetition states that things are repeated continuously to highlight the importance of the subject matter. God wants us to understand that obeying our parents is essential to our future. This subject is not up for a vote; it is of supreme importance that this commandment is a practice of our lives.

Today, many parents christen or dedicate their children without completely understanding the responsibility and commitment that comes with that dedication ceremony. Many parents only see baby christenings as an opportunity to get their children dressed up in elaborate christening outfits. There is nothing wrong with this idea of considering this a special event, but there is more to this event than outfits and photos. The significance of this ceremony is to give thanks to God for allowing that child to be born. Still, more importantly, this is an opportunity for parents and Godparents to rededicate their homes and lives to God. This is an opportunity for pastors and spiritual fathers to urge parents to bring their children up

Proverbs 16:31: *"The hoary head is a crown of glory, if it be found in the way of righteousness."*

Proverbs 20:29: *"The glory of young men is their strength: and the beauty of old men is the grey head."*

Growing up in the sixties, I was taught to recognize white, gray, silver, and balding as indicators of wisdom and experience. As a result, I had preset boundaries I knew not to cross in engaging with my elders. I remember when the late Bishop George A. Wallace would visit my family when I was still a child. In those days, people were encouraged to hold pastors and spiritual leaders in high regard. My parents and grandmother would practically lay out the red carpet of special treatment for him.

In how the children interacted with Elisha, it is obvious the principles of honor and respect were violated, and it brought dreadful results to the lives of the children who mocked the aging prophet.

Leviticus 19:32 says, "*Thou shalt rise up before the hoary head, and honor the face of the old man, and fear thy God: I am the Lord.*"

In Old Testament times, harsh consequences came to those who did not respect their elders. These consequences were not meant to address the point of dishonor but also God's displeasure for the spirit behind the act of dishonor.

Deuteronomy 21:18-21: *"If a man have a stubborn and rebellious son, which will not obey the voice of his father, or the voice of his mother, and that, when they have chastened him, will not hearken unto them: Then shall his father and his mother lay hold on him, and bring him out unto the elders of his city, and unto the gate of his place; And they shall say unto the elders of his city, This our son is stubborn and rebellious, he will not obey our voice; he is a glutton and a drunkard. And all the men of his city shall stone him with stones, that he die: so shalt thou put evil away from among you; and all Israel shall hear, and fear."*

I do not propose that we perpetuate violence, but I do believe that even today, we must give deference to the elderly, especially those who are faithful and loyal to the things of God. These are our spiritual fathers and mothers who have begotten us in the Lord. We should not so easily forget the sacrifices and the labor of older saints. In many Christian circles, there is the continual message to forget the past, but it is almost impossible to chart the future without understanding the treasured memories of the past.

It is important to note that Elisha called the bears out of the woods to devour the children, but their path of wayward behavior led to their destruction. When there is a failure to care for and honor our elderly, it exposes us to unwanted dangers that otherwise could have been avoided.

I believe Psalm 71:18 is the cry of many of our saints who have toiled and labored in the vineyard of the Lord, *"Now also when I am old and grey headed, O God, forsake me not; until I have shewed thy strength unto this generation, and thy power to everyone that is to come."*

Many of our elderly saints have so much to give but so little opportunity to share. They are the seasoned prayer warriors and intercessors that our churches so desperately need in these times. I thank God for the saints who took the time to lay hands on me and pray for my salvation. Sincere spiritual mothers and fathers wanted to see me succeed and not succumb to the enemy's devices had set for my life.

I will never forget the day Bishop Jocelyn Williams, Pastor Emeritus of the Rehoboth Church of God, and his wife called my wife and me to meet him at the church. I knew he was preparing to leave, but I did not realize it would be that soon. On that Wednesday, I knelt at the altar, and he laid his hands on me, imparting wisdom, interceding on my behalf with a heartfelt prayer and admonishment. There was no fanfare or applause because the sanctuary was empty. It was indeed a powerful moment, one I liken to a Moses laying hands on Joshua. I will forever be grateful for both his and Lady William's prayers of support.

Rehoboam was the son of King Solomon. Although Rehoboam was the heir apparent to secede the throne after his father's death, he failed to gain the favor of the people because he was unwilling to listen to sound advice from the elders. This was the missing factor in Rehoboam's ascension to the throne.

We read in 1 Kings 12 that Jeroboam, who had formerly been placed in charge of the house of Joseph under the reign of King Solomon but was later exiled by King Solomon, returns to Jerusalem.

When the elders hear of his return, they immediately call upon Jeroboam to assist with the transition process of Rehoboam becoming king after King Solomon's passing.

Rehoboam had within his grasp the ability to make decisions that could have solidified the kingdom of Israel under his leadership. But his failure to honor the counsel of his elders would ultimately lead to his failure.

> 1 Kings 12:3-16: *"That they sent and called him. And Jeroboam and all the congregation of Israel came, and spake unto Rehoboam, saying, Thy father made our yoke grievous: now therefore make thou the grievous service of thy father, and his heavy yoke which he put upon us, lighter, and we will serve thee. And he said unto them, Depart yet for three days, then come again to me. And the people departed.*
>
> *And king Rehoboam consulted with the old men, that stood before Solomon his father while he yet lived, and said, How do ye advise that I may answer this people? And they spake unto him, saying, If thou wilt be a servant unto this people this day, and wilt serve them, and answer them, and speak good words to them, then they will be thy servants forever. But he forsook the counsel of the old men, which they had given him, and consulted with the young men that were grown up with him, and which stood before him:*
>
> *And he said unto them, What counsel give ye that we may answer this people, who have spoken to me, saying, Make the yoke which thy father did put upon us lighter? And the young men that were grown up with*

him spake unto him, saying, Thus shalt thou speak unto this people that spake unto thee, saying, Thy father made our yoke heavy, but make thou it lighter unto us; thus shalt thou say unto them, My little finger shall be thicker than my father's loins. And now whereas my father did lade you with a heavy yoke, I will add to your yoke: my father hath chastised you with whips, but I will chastise you with scorpions.

So Jeroboam and all the people came to Rehoboam the third day, as the king had appointed, saying, Come to me again the third day. And the king answered the people roughly and forsook the old men's counsel that they gave him; And spake to them after the counsel of the young men, saying, My father made your yoke heavy, and I will add to your yoke: my father also chastised you with whips, but I will chastise you with scorpions.

Wherefore the king hearkened not unto the people; for the cause was from the Lord, that he might perform his saying, which the Lord spake by Ahijah the Shilonite unto Jeroboam the son of Nebat. So when all Israel saw that the king hearkened not unto them, the people answered the king, saying, What portion have we in David? neither have we inheritance in the son of Jesse: to your tents, O Israel: now see to thine own house, David. So Israel departed unto their tents" (KJV, 1998).

As the story goes, the congregation thought that the taxes King Solomon had levied upon the people during his reign were excessive. The people were optimistic that with new leadership taking the throne, there might be some leniency given in that regard. The first thing Rehoboam does is ask Jeroboam and the congregation to give him three days to deliberate the matter.

During the three days, Rehoboam consulted with the older men who had counseled his father, Solomon. The elders advised him to speak good words to the people and lighten the load to be willing and loyal subjects. However, the Bible says he forsook the counsel of the older men. There are times when youthfulness can bring brashness and a spirit of stubbornness. Rehoboam would soon learn that not honoring the counsel of the elders was a critical misstep.

Rehoboam then reaches to his peers for advice. Unlike the older men, the young men had not heard the cries of the people and therefore did not understand what needed to be done. The young men were presumptuous, arrogant, and vain, while the older men acted with wisdom and prudence. The young men said, "*Thus shalt thou speak unto this that spake unto thee, saying, Thy father made our yoke heavy, but make thou it lighter unto us; thus shalt thou say unto them, My little finger shall be thicker than my father's loins. And now whereas my father did lade you with a heavy yoke: I will add to your yoke: my father hath chastised you with whips, but I will chastise you with scorpions*" (1 Kings 12:10-11).

The young men lacked tack and compassion. Their words were pointed and harsh. Rehoboam chose to listen to the inexperience of their youth rather than heed the wisdom of the older men's experience. When the third day came, Rehoboam received the men with the younger men's words that were spoken to him. As a response to Rehoboam's brashness, the people revolted and divorced themselves from the leadership of Rehoboam. The kingdom was split into two. Now what once was one nation became two: The Northern Kingdom and The Southern Kingdom.

How often do we hear of Church splits that occur out of a disgruntled faction that disagrees with the direction of the congregation's leadership? In this case, Rehoboam was at fault because he refused to heed the counsel of the elders. I cannot count the number of mistakes I would have made in ministry had I not heeded the warnings of the spiritual fathers. I must admit, sometimes their words were bitter to my ears, but the outcome would be sweet to my spirit.

The spirit of Rehoboam is still heavily present. I have heard countless stories of older pastors who attempted to guide spiritual sons and daughters in the ministry; and how the younger ministers resisted their counsel and sought to set off on their paths that many times led to disaster and frustration.

> Proverbs 23:22-24: *"Hearken unto thy father that begat thee and despise not thy mother when she is old. Buy the truth, and sell it not; also wisdom, and instruction, and understanding. The father of the righteous shall greatly rejoice: and he that begetteth a wise child shall have joy of him."*

> Proverbs 1:8: *"My son, hear the instruction of thy father, and forsake not the law of thy mother."*

> Proverbs 4:1: *"Hear, ye children, the instruction of a father, and*

attend to know understanding."

1 Peter 5:5: *"Likewise, ye younger, submit yourselves unto the elder. Yea, all of you be subject one to another, and be clothed with humility: for God resisteth the proud, and giveth grace to the humble."*

I have been alive long enough to have lived on both sides of the spectrum; one as a young man being instructed by older men and now as an older man speaking into the lives of many young men and women of God who call on me for counsel. I have learned over time that spiritual fathers and children have equal parts to play in this spiritual connection. Ephesians 6:4 says, "*And, ye fathers, provoke not your children to wrath, but bring them up in the nurture and admonish of the Lord.*"

The word nurture means care, loving support, longsuffering, and compassionate mercy. This is needed in the lives of spiritual children. Just as I have seen sons and daughters deeply wound their spiritual fathers out of rebellion and willful disobedience, I have also seen spiritual fathers alienate and isolate their sons as David isolated Absalom.

As spiritual fathers, we have to be mature enough to be comfortable with our own abilities and anointing so that the 'Elishas' of our day come into our lives. We must be ready to embrace them and help propel them into their prophetic destiny. Two of the greatest dangers that many times overtake the spirit of spiritual fathers are insecurity and selfishness. We *must* be willing to impart to others what God has given us. We *must* have the desire to see the next generation's success supersede ours.

I will never forget the words my father spoke to me before he went to his eternal reward in glory, *"My prayer for you is that you would go where I have never gone and that you will do what I have never done."* It was as if he spoke destiny into my life with his final words. The prophetic words that were said to me that day have become my reality. I want to prayerfully pass those words on to my children and hopefully to my grandchildren.

This must have been the prayer of Elijah as he raised up spiritual sons in Ramah, the place known as the school of the prophets. My prayer today is that more and more spiritual fathers and mothers will breathe life into this generation. Sons and daughters are waiting and crying out for God to give them spiritual fathers to emulate and receive godly wisdom. Will you be counted among those who respond to this cry? Will you take up the mantle and invest your life in someone else?

Chapter 10

Absence of a Father's Discipline in Worship

I am always fascinated with the story of David, especially the scene where David is bringing the Ark of the Covenant out of the house of Obededom as he is offering up sacrifices to God. The Bible says David brings the Ark with gladness, and he begins to dance before the Lord with all of his might.

> 2 Samuel 6:15-16, *"So David and all the house of Israel brought up the ark of the Lord with shouting, and with the sound of the trumpet. And as the ark of the Lord came into the city of David, Michal Saul's daughter looked through a window, and saw King David leaping and dancing before the Lord; and she despised him in her heart."*

David was a man of great courage and resilience who unashamedly led his nation into a time of praise and worship. Our world needs to see this example; men forgetting about their titles and positions and wholly giving themselves in worship to God. Where there is an absence of men submitted in worship to God, there is an open gate for the people to become seduced by other gods, bringing disease, destruction, and death.

Another example of a man giving devoted worship to God is found in the story of Abraham and Isaac. God asks Abraham to offer up his son as an offering to Him. After waiting years for the birth of his promised seed, Abraham now has the heart-wrenching

Children are arrows in our hands. An archer must be skillful in knowing how to handle the bow. At the same time, he has to understand that if he wants to hit his desired target, he must be steady with the bow and precise in his aim. How often do we, as parents, miss valuable opportunities to propel our children forward when we do not seek the Lord for their destiny? When we fail to accept investing spiritual truth as an important mandate, we fail to provide them the best foundation for withstanding and navigating the vicissitudes of life.

Job, another model for a strong spiritual father, sets this example. The Bible says he sanctified his children before the Lord (Job 1:5). No, we cannot protect our children from every calamity that might befall them. But if we offer them to God, it is an opportunity to give them over to God's direction and divine protection.

Parents must take the initiative to fulfill our responsibility by interceding for the precious gifts God has placed in their hands and release them forward like the arrows in a skilled archer's hand. The weapon of prayer is a vital and powerful tool in shaping our children's future, so why is it so seldom used? Too often, it is kept in the arsenal of relics that are only utilized in crisis. Fathers, we need to dust off our storage bags and release the weapon of prayer against the enemies of our children's destiny and purpose.

When we look at this divine edict from God, we can quickly see the Abraham and Isaac story as a typology or a precursor to God giving His only Son for us that we might have eternal life. Sometimes God will use our life as a model of things to come so others who come after us will have an example to follow.

In his arduous journey climbing up Mount Moriah, Abraham had many opportunities to change his mind and disobey the command, but he persevered. Abraham could have turned back after reaching his destination, but instead, he said to his servants, *"Wait here while the lad and I will go and worship"* (Genesis 22:5).

When we emphatically obey the voice of God, it sets us up for more incredible things to come. The test was to give Abraham a testimony of God's faithfulness, to prove that God can be trusted even in the conflicting times of our lives.

Children see their fathers as role models. I recall seeing my father waking up at 4:30 a.m. in the morning to prepare to go to work as a mail carrier for the United States Post Office. On one occasion, my father shared how he had gotten bitten by a dog. On another occasion how he had to deal with difficult people who harassed mail carriers. Yet because of his commitment to his family, he went to work daily until he was forced to retire due to health concerns. Not only was my father a mail carrier, but he was also a pastor. I distinctly remember him pastoring a church that was located over two hours away from home. The drive was already an exhausting and difficult one that was exasperated by the fact that he would make this drive after working long hours in the grueling Florida sun.

My father was a dedicated pastor who extended himself as much as possible to his congregants. My father, Jonathan Ramsey Sr., would work his regular job, come home in the afternoon on a Wednesday, rest for 45 minutes, get right back on the road and drive to the church. My father was dedicated beyond words. His example is my model for ministry.

One image that always stands out in my mind is my father in the front room on his knees in prayer. I would often wake up in the middle of the night and find him in this act of worship. I also reflect on the many mornings and evenings when my father would call the family together for family devotion. Those images of worship and devotion to God left indelible imprints on my heart.

For as much as our children see us facing the rigors of life to provide for them, they should even more so see us in acts of worship, giving praise to God for His manifold blessings. So many great leaders have shared their fathers' impact on them because of their devotion to God. Regrettably, at the same time, too many children are left without those images.

Abraham told his servants that he and his son were going to worship. Abraham did not say that he and his son were going up to make a sacrifice. Perhaps that would be assumed, but the thought of going up and worshipping with his son is gripping. Some fathers prioritize that their children are dressed and out to church bright and early on Sunday morning. However, today, many of the sports activities that our children are engaged in are primarily held on

Sunday mornings. I believe this is by intentional design, a distraction to cause our children to miss out on the vital foundational principle of worship to God.

I would allow my sons to attend activities on Sunday. However, they were required to attend church either before or after the activity. When our children see us as fathers putting the secular before the spiritual, it sends the wrong message about their relationship with God. This is something that I had to check myself on constantly. I conclude that worship is more essential to our children's futures than anything else we can offer them.

When I look further into this account of Abraham and Isaac traveling up the terrain of Mount Moriah, I can vividly envision Isaac asking his father the million-dollar question, *"Behold the fire and the wood: but where is the burnt offering?"* (Genesis 22:7). Perhaps Isaac had seen his father go through this process countless times, but there was always a sacrifice on those occasions. However, this time something was missing. Abraham, without knowing the outcome, responded with such spiritual sensitivity. He said, *"God will provide himself a lamb for a burnt offering"* (Genesis 22:8). Abraham was prepared to follow God's command to the letter.

Look at the picture of obedience that is depicted in this process. We see young Isaac trusting the words of his natural father that there would be a lamb for the sacrifice, not knowing that he was the lamb. Then we have the picture of Abraham trusting his Heavenly Father with the outcome of what he was requested to do.

Children follow the examples of what they see modeled by their parents. There are always things that we see in ourselves that are replayed in the lives of our children. As it relates to my father and me, I picked up his love for staying up late and watching television. I see that habit developed in my children in their adulthood. In this day and time, we cannot say *"do as I say and not as I do."* Our children are taking mental notes and will follow in our steps.

Abraham's example demonstrates that worship requires obedience. Not only is obedience essential to worship, but equally important is the exercising of your faith in worship. Your faith in God takes you to a level of worship that is otherwise naturally unattainable. Abraham believed God so much that he said to the servant, *"I and the lad will go, worship, and come again to you."* Abraham believed the same God Who commanded him to offer up his only son Isaac was also able to raise Isaac again, if necessary. Abraham displayed total faith in God.

Faith can be defined as believing in God without evidence. Hebrews 11:1 says, *"Now faith is the substance of things hoped for, the evidence of things not seen."*

Abraham put faith into action when he pursued the will of God by taking Isaac up to Moriah, but the process of faith would not have been complete without following through with supporting action.

Just as God had instructed, Abraham prepared the wood for

the sacrifice. He had the stave laid in its proper place. It was then time for him to tie his son up to become the living sacrifice. Can you imagine the heart-breaking thoughts that must have run through the mind of Abraham? Think about the countless times you have faced inner turmoil over challenging things that you felt were necessary but costly. This particular action, the offering of Isaac, was going to be a tremendous step of faith. The son of promise was laid out on the altar prepared for sacrifice.

I can remember back in the late 70s and the early 80s as my father continued to fulfill the difficult task of pastoring the church. This is after he had experienced some health challenges and was in his doctor's care. Despite my father's medication, he had another setback that left him paralyzed on one side of his body. It was very difficult for me. Some moments were difficult to reconcile because I saw a faithful man who loved God with all his heart lying sick in the bed. But then I saw his faith in action at a time of crisis. That was faith at another level.

Weeks after being stricken with paralysis, my father was up walking and testifying to the miraculous power of God and how He had restored his mobility. One afternoon, while he lay in the hospital, one of the deacons from the church came to pray for him. My father believed that if God allowed this situation to occur in his life, then God could also raise him up. God did just that. It is one thing for our children to hear us speak about faith, but it leaves a permanent impression when they see us standing in faith.

The scriptures do not indicate any more conversation between Isaac and Abraham over the process of the offering of the sacrifice. Isaac watched his father tying him up. They were alone on the top of a mountain, and just as Abraham had to have faith in God, Isaac had to have faith in his father.

The story ends with Isaac on the altar and Abraham ready to come down with the stave in his hand to slay Isaac. But the Lord intervened, and Abraham was presented with a ram instead of his son as a sacrifice.

How committed are we to worship? Currently, our nation and our world are faced with the challenge of fighting a disease that has ravished the lives of millions of people across the globe. Now is the time to seek the face of God in prayer and worship.

> 2 Chronicles 7:14, *"If my people, which are called by my name, shall humble themselves, and pray, and seek my face, and turn from their wicked ways; then will I hear from heaven, and will forgive their sin, and will heal their land."*

Our world needs the healing touch of God. I wonder what would happen if all the men on earth fell on their faces before God and prayed a prayer of repentance. I believe there would be a mighty answer from Heaven, one of redemption, restoration, and revival.

There is a need for men to turn to God with committed hearts and dedicated worship. In this time of a pandemic, churches that were once flooded with people are now either empty or managed by the few who are allowed to participate. But that does not stop worship. Worship takes place in the hearts of men to the God of heaven.

Psalm 103:1 says, *"Bless the Lord, O my soul: and all that is within me, bless his holy name."*

This is the praise that must come from our mouths at this critical time in our history. Fathers need to be wholeheartedly lifting up holy hands in praise to God. It is often said that men are detached when it comes to expressing emotion, especially in worship. But I believe that we change that paradigm because this generation needs to see paternal role models who are radical in their worship. They need to see men who are not intimidated by showing affection and appreciation to the God of Heaven for His manifold blessings toward us. Psalm 107:8 says, "*Oh that men would praise the Lord for his goodness, and for his wonderful works to the children of men!*"

I believe this was Abraham's intent in faithfully carrying out the sacrificial act. He was so committed to the process that only a voice from heaven prevented him from completing his assignment. Abraham's act of worship was an act of supreme sacrifice to God his Creator.

The angel tells Abraham not to lay his hands on his son to harm him. Then the words that follow are words that speak to the depth of Abraham's commitment to God. God declares "*Now I know that thou fearest God, seeing that thou has not withheld thy son, thine only son from me"* (Genesis 22:12).

Abraham was willing to sacrifice the dearest thing to him. Isaac represented his legacy, the covenant God had made to him, and the promised seed that nations would come forth from Abraham's obedience. His faith and commitment paid off.

It was in that moment of verbal approval from God that a miracle took place. The Bible says Abraham lifted up his eyes and looked, and there to his amazement, he finds a ram caught in a thicket (Genesis 22:13). I believe Abraham was relieved because he took the ram and offered him a burnt sacrifice instead of his son. The angel speaking could have been a reprieve, but the ram was a guarantee that God had another plan in store for Abraham.

Abraham called the name of the place Jehovah-Jireh. It was the place the Lord provided a sacrifice. This is a testimony to us today that God will provide when we obey God's commandments.

I saw this continually in my family's life as my father followed the Lord. It was challenging for us to travel two hours to church and sometimes stay for the weekend. We did not leave until the Sunday night service was over. However, God always provided a place for us to stay, food to eat, and enough time for my sisters and me to complete our classwork. We excelled in all the things we set our hands to because my father's faithfulness and commitment to God released a blessing for us to succeed.

Abraham's life is a model for all fathers to follow. Though we are not called to physically sacrifice our children on an altar, it is the will of our Heavenly Father that we present our bodies a living sacrifice, holy and acceptable to God, which is our reasonable service (Romans 12:1). That type of sacrifice is what provokes the hand of God and causes blessings to overflow in the lives of our children. This is something that can be reciprocated in every family's life as fathers give themselves wholly to the plan and purpose of God. Abraham's sacrifice in worship is still affecting generations today and beyond. Like Abraham, fathers today can become an army of worshippers who change the trajectory of our children for generations to come.

One of the images the enemy of our purpose hates to see is men of God lifting holy hands in worship to God. Throughout scripture, we see how when men worship God, breakthroughs, and deliverance occur; strongholds are broken down, and many the dreams and hopes of many are fulfilled. When Adam fell in the Garden, one of Satan's purposes was to take man away from the presence and peace of God. It is often said that only weak men worship, but on the contrary, it takes a strong man to submit himself to God in a position of worship.

> Psalm 107:31: *"Oh that men would praise the Lord for his goodness, and for his wonderful works to the children of men!"*

There is a need for a paradigm shift in our world today. Rather than men portraying strength through war and violence, we need to see men in total submission giving worship and praise to

God. For it is in this act that real strength, good character, and truth are displayed.

Chapter 11

Absence of a Father's Legacy

In 2007, Tyler Perry wrote and directed a movie entitled *Daddy's Little Girls* (Perry, n.d.). The film depicted a courageous father willing to put his life on the line to protect his children from their drug-dealing mother, who had won custody of them in court. As the children's protector, he stood up to a notorious gangster while running the risk of being reincarcerated. He falls in love with an attorney who, in the end, helps him secure legal custody of his children. *Daddy's Little Girls* revealed a father's deep love for his daughters and the limits a father will go through to display that love.

I can remember holding my daughter in my arms, rocking her to sleep when she was only a couple of months old. She would be crying in the middle of the night, finding it difficult to fall asleep. My wife and I would take turns staying awake with her until she fell asleep. The care and the love that I was able to provide for her as a father began to wedge a bond between us that continues today.

When my daughter went off to college, she wrote me a passionate letter thanking me for being a good father. That letter meant more to me than any award or accolade that I had attained. Those words that my daughter shared remind me of the legacy my father left for me, and that is the example I want to go for my children.

Proverbs 13:22 reads, *"A good man leaves an inheritance for his children."*

One of the things I most admired about my father was his commitment and loyalty to God and his family. As I said earlier, my father would go out to work sometimes at 4:30 in the morning and return home around 4:00 p.m. He would be so tired from the day and needing to rest. Yet, within minutes of arriving home, he would be up and ready to get on the highway, traveling over two hundred miles roundtrip to a 25-member congregation that he pastored. For my father, it was not about the size of the congregation or about the strenuous job he had as a mail carrier for the United States Post Office; it was about his love for God and his family.

My father shared with us the reason why he made the sacrifices he made. He stated it was about making life better for his children and their future. He once said to me, *"You would do things I never had the opportunity to do; go places I never had the opportunity to travel to."* That statement still resonates with me today. It has inspired me to keep moving forward. My father may not have left his children millions of dollars, but he did go with us is a legacy of commitment and sacrifice that outweighs the value of silver and gold.

In the book of Deuteronomy, we are told the story of the daughters of Zelophehad. It was time for Moses to begin to distribute the inheritance of the land to each tribe and family of the children of Israel. However, when it came to the property of Zelophehad, there was a problem. Zelophehad had no sons, only daughters. Based on the law at that time, upon a person's death, their inheritance would be passed onto the eldest son if he were alive, or one of the other sons, in order according to age. It was the son that would carry on the name of the father. However, the daughters would receive a dowry at the time of their wedding. A dowry is defined as property or money a bride brings to her husband on their marriage date.

While the bride price or bride service is a payment by the groom or his family to the bride's parents, dowry is the wealth transferred from the bride's family to the groom or his family, ostensibly for the bride. In the case of the daughters of Zelophehad, since there were no brothers, the inheritance was now set to go to the next male relative in line. There were no actual provisions for a legacy for the daughter if the father dies.

The culture of that day was male dominant. Women were in many ways relegated to a role of servility. It was almost as if the woman's place was to be silent unless someone was speaking to her. For these young women to stand up for themselves was to risk rejection, possible reprimand, and retribution. However, the daughters of Zelophehad were courageous and took that risk (Numbers 27:1-5).

Courage is defined as the quality of mind or spirit that enables a person to face difficulty. President Theodore Roosevelt once said, "Courage is not having the strength to go on, it's going on when you don't have the strength." In other words, someone who has courage might not be fearless, but they have the moral strength to venture out.

We can see this type of courage in the late '50s and the early 60's when women picketed, held stand-ins, and had public forums advocating for the right to vote. Because of the heroic efforts of women like Eleanor Roosevelt and Esther Peterson, who headed the first Women's Commission, rights and privileges were secured for women who otherwise would have been withheld.

Throughout history, we have had women who displayed heroic courage and have made their mark on history.

Malala Yousafzai

"When the whole world is silent, even one voice becomes powerful."

Malala Yousafzai courageously campaigned for equal education for girls in Pakistan from a very young age, blogging anonymously for the British Broadcast Company (BBC News) as a child. When she was just 15, Yousafzai was shot in the head by a member of the Taliban while traveling home from school in a targeted attack. She miraculously survived the attack and, at just 17, became the youngest person to ever win the Nobel Peace Prize. Yousafzai never let the attack deter her bravery and uses her global platform to advocate for girls' education. Her achievements are countless, and being a UN Messenger for Peace and the world's youngest Nobel laureate, Yousafzai was recently accepted into Oxford University to study Philosophy, Politics, and Economics (PPE). Ban Ki-Moon, UN Secretary-General, describes her as *"a brave and gentle advocate of peace who through the simple act of going to school became a global teacher."*

Amelia Earhart

"Women must try to do things as men have tried. When they fail, their failure must be but a challenge to others."

A true pioneer, Amelia Earhart was only the sixth woman in the world to own a pilot's license. Her trailblazing spirit led her to be the first female aviator to fly solo across the Atlantic in 1928. Earhart never let fear get the better of her and described anxieties as "paper tigers." Although Earhart disappeared during an attempt to circumnavigate the globe in 1937, her bravery and innovation make her an inspiration to women everywhere, even 80 years later (Haddrick, 2018).

Rosa Parks

"I have learned over the years that when one's mind is made up, this diminishes fear; knowing what must be done does away with fear."

In 1955, Rosa Parks became a key figure in the Civil Rights movement when, in her own words, *"all [she] was doing was trying to get home from work."* When traveling home from work, a white passenger demanded Parks give up her seat, to which she replied, *"No."* This single reply became the catalyst for a 381-day bus boycott, resulting in a law repealing bus segregation. The day of Parks' arrest is now honored as Rosa Parks Day, cementing her legacy as the First Lady of the Civil Rights (Haddrick, 2018).

Audrey Hepburn

"Nothing is impossible; the word itself says 'I'm possible!"

Although she is perhaps best remembered for her incredible beauty and inimitable style, Audrey Hepburn also led a courageous life. Hepburn grew up in Arnhem, the Netherlands, and gave private, silent ballet recitals to raise money for the Dutch resistance during the Nazi occupation. As a result of the Nazi occupation, Hepburn spent much of her childhood impoverished and malnourished. She also risked her life transporting messages and money to local resistance contact Hepburn never forgot the kindness and aid she received during the liberation and spent her later years working as a committed ambassador to UNICEF (Aksu, 2020).

Anne Frank

"How wonderful it is that nobody need wait a single moment before starting to improve the world" (Resources That Inform, and Equip Foster Parents, 2018).

The famous diarist behind The Diary of a Young Girl, Anne Frank, began writing about her experiences as a Jewish girl in Nazi-occupied Amsterdam on her 13th birthday. The diary offers a poignant insight into her life in the secret annex, living in constant fear of discovery. Frank died at just 15 in the Bergen-Belsen concentration camp. Although many passages reflect the overwhelming despair of the period, her diary is remarkable for its optimism, hope, and love for mankind. Frank credits her emotional resilience and capacity to forgive to *"inward strength and plenty of courage"* (Haddrick, 2018).

It takes courage for women to stand up and dare to forge forward to achieve their highest potential, so it was the case of the daughters of Zelophehad. Although they did not have a father to speak up for them, or a brother to provide for them, they dared to stand up for their rights.

These daughters of Zelophehad not only had courage, but they portrayed the strong character as well. Moses was a great leader who the people of Israel held in high regard. For these young women to come into the presence of Moses with a request that could alter how the distribution of land would be done took great strength. Most people faced with similar circumstances would defer to living with the status quo. But the daughters of Zelophehad stood up and made their case without being intimidated by the magnitude of the moment. Once they decided to move forward with their plan, there was no turning back. They were standing up for what they knew was rightfully theirs—something that would have otherwise been forfeited by remaining silent.

They dared to ask, *"Why should the name of our father be done away from among his family because he hath no son? Give unto us, therefore, a possession among the brethren of our father"* (Numbers 27:4).

As fathers, we should always be diligent about providing a legacy for our children.

Two years ago, I had the privilege of speaking at my grandfather's funeral. He was a man who seemed larger than life. He would always talk about the possibility of his children and grandchildren coming back to Heath Springs, South Carolina. Mr. Gonze Lee Twitty had mapped out acres of land that he had accumulated for this purpose. It was his legacy of love to generations that would outlive himself.

A good man leaveth an inheritance for his children's children (Szalavitz, 2010).

Zelophehad's daughters saw that there would not be an inheritance for them, so they had to take courage and cry out for what they felt was rightfully theirs.

When we look at the declarative way the young women spoke up for them, we can demonstrate their character's power. *"Give unto us therefore a possession among the brethren of our father"* (Numbers 27:4). Although they spoke with boldness and confidence, they were in no way disrespectful to Moses or the elders. The daughters of Zelophehad realized if they did not stand up for themselves, no one else would.

These women dared to act and a character that displayed strength. But these young women were also committed to the cause. The word commitment is defined as dedicated, having a sense of devotion, faithfulness to a purpose.

Because of these women's commitment, Moses had to take notice of their plea. Moses immediately interceded to God on behalf of these women (Numbers 27:5). There are times when our earthly fathers fail to make provisions for us, but our Heavenly Father intentionally places people in our lives to act on our behalf. In this case, it was the leader of Israel, Moses. However, it was not Moses' response alone that made the difference, but God Almighty.

> Numbers 27:7: *"The daughters of Zelophehad speak right: thou shalt surely give them a possession of an inheritance among their father's brethren; and thou shalt cause the inheritance of their father to pass unto them."*

When Moses brought the daughters of Zelophehad complaint before the Lord, God corrected the unfair position that these girls were placed in (Numbers 27:7).

How often is it within our power to right social injustices, but we remain silent because it may not directly affect us? Today, we have sons and daughters who possess extraordinary abilities and possibilities. Still, there are not enough fathers who will speak up on behalf of those powerless to act for themselves. We have political, judicial, and even religious institutions that force our younger generations to forfeit opportunities that their inaction would have otherwise afforded them.

God instructed Moses to set things in order so that the

daughters of Zelophehad could have what rightfully belonged to them.

As spiritual fathers, we must release our children into their destinies with the greatest investment we can give them— a legacy of love, a legacy of commitment, and a legacy of prosperity. This is exactly what Job did.

After Job *(another biblical figure)* experienced one of the most tragic periods of suffering, God blessed him to gain double blessings for his pain. As a part of his restoration process, God blessed him with seven more sons and three daughters. The Bible says of Job's daughters that they were the fairest women in the land. But the statement that catches my attention the most is, *"And their father gave them inheritance among their brethren"* (Job 42:10-15). That is a powerful picture of women being given the same dignity and value that men freely receive.

We often see women being exploited for their beauty and treated as a lower creation than men. Today we know this exploitation in tabloid magazines where women are used as objects for merchandising, and even more degrading, some women are kidnapped and trafficked across international lines. Many laws have been put in place to prevent such practices, but most cases against such charges are never followed through because of loopholes in the legal system.

This travesty that takes place every day in America highlights the plight many women face in dominant male environments. We see this devaluing of women even in the workplace where women work the same jobs as men but are paid at a lower rate than men. Statistically, women are paid at a rate of 17.7% less than men for the same job, as reported by Business Insider (Sheth S., Hoff, M., Ward, M., & Tyson, T., 2021)

Women everywhere are crying out for their father's inheritance, but they are left out of the distribution of assets in many cases. Where would the daughters of Zelophehad have ended up if they had not spoken up for themselves? They would have probably ended up in a position of hoping and wishing that some male suitor would deem them worthy of being taken as his wife. This is an unfair tradeoff for the happiness and success that many women have to settle for when they want their fair access to legacy. Spiritual fathers must ensure that their daughters never have to be subjugated to this treatment. This is done by providing an adequate legacy for their inheritance.

When we look at the difference in what happened in the story of the daughters of Zelophehad and the daughters of Job, we can quickly identify the need for spiritual fathers to leave an inheritance for their sons and daughters. Too often, our daughters are left to the subjectivity of a man's love or favor, and they are not given the same opportunities to shape their paths. Job's sons *and* daughters both had a sense of security in looking at their future.

Much of the wealth that most Americans have amassed is

inherited wealth. This affirms the importance of passing on a legacy. *"A 2017 study published by Thomas Pickett and colleagues estimated that in 2010, about 60 percent of the private wealth held in the United States had been inherited, rather than worked for"* (Ingrahm, 2019).

"Of the total wealth of the population, Kessler and Masson estimated that 35 percent originated from inheritances or gifts. Among those who had reported receiving an intergenerational transfer (who were about two and a half times richer than the average household), the corresponding proportion was 40 percent" (Wolff, 2011).

Spiritual fathers and mothers have so much to offer to the next generation. Although much of the financial wealth is in the hands of the few, the wealth of knowledge and wisdom that has been amassed through our years of experience and learning is just as valuable. God had a blessed job to have the material wealth to pass on to his children. But whatever little or much we possess, we must be willing to invest it in the lives of spiritual sons and daughters.

One of the most memorable occasions in my life was the day I drove my family to Kannapolis, North Carolina, for a summer vacation. This city is significant because it is where my father and mother met for the first time while in high school. Secondly, it was the city that my grandfather, Bishop John Alfred Ramsey, had pastored a small church on the hill some forty years prior. I must note that my paternal grandfather died before I was born, but I would see legacy in action on that day.

One of the men, who had been a deacon at the church where my grandfather had pastored some years ago, had kept my grandfather's *grip* or what we today call his attaché' case as a memorial. On that day, Brother Carson brought the grip out from the storage place where he had kept it for all of those years and presented it to me. I was overwhelmed and, at the same time, very proud that I now had a prize possession of my grandfather's. Although I never heard him preach or ever got to be in his presence, having his grip spoke volumes in my life. That is what legacy is all about. Today, that grip sits in my office as a reminder of the legacy of ministry that has been passed on to me. To God be the glory.

Chapter 12

Making the Connection

In the summer of 1980-81, a group of college students from Lee University had the opportunity to serve on a mission team evangelizing in Tallahassee and Lake City, Florida. Evangelist Betty Haynie led the group. She was a fiery and determined prayer warrior who deeply loved what she did, and she expected no less from the people who worked alongside her.

During that summer, I learned more about the power and the work of the Holy Spirit than I had ever known before. Evangelist Haynie had us spend hours in prayer and intercession. She taught us what it meant to pray in the Spirit as the spirit of God gave utterance. When we finished our times of prayer, it felt as if we had literally touched heaven or as if heaven had come down to us. These were special times of prayer that prepared our hearts for what God was going to do in our midst.

Those moments were so impactful and have helped define my understanding of ministry. Those summer meetings gave birth to two churches and set ablaze spiritual sons and daughters for the cause of Christ.

Evangelist Betty Haynie displayed characteristics that made her effective in leading and helping the group develop spiritual depth. Evangelist Haynie led with patience in dealing with our inconsistencies and immaturity. Although we made many mistakes along the way, she chose not to give up on us prematurely. Lovingly she corrected us and then showed us the proper way of how to conduct ourselves.

Patience is absent in the approach that many spiritual fathers utilize to teach those they lead. Patience requires you to recognize that no one is perfect. It challenges us to see our frailties and weaknesses in the areas that we still have growth. The Scriptures admonish us to be patient with others through their challenges:

> 1 Corinthians 10:12: *"Wherefore let him that thinketh he standeth take heed lest he fall."*

> Galatians 6:1: *"Brothers and sisters, if someone is caught in a sin, you who live by the Spirit should restore that person gently. But watch yourselves, or you also may be tempted."*

Author and Behavioral Scientist Steve Maraboli put it like this, *"Think of the patience God has had for you and let it resonate to others. If you want a more patient world, let patience be your motto."*

It was not only Evangelist Haynie's patience that drew the attention of those who followed her, but it was her passion for what she believed. When unfortunate circumstances appeared, she did not allow that to deter her from her assignment.

One day while we were out witnessing in the community, she stopped by the home of a young lady she had previously known. This particular girl shared with us her reasoning for not continuing in her relationship with God. But as the conversation progressed and Evangelist Haynie continued to engage, that same young lady began to surrender her heart and life back to God. That same week, the young lady attended multiple services. This young lady's restoration was a direct result of Reverend Haynie's passion for lost souls. Let us look at some verses that speak to the importance of soul-winning:

> Proverbs 10:5: *"He that gathereth in summer is a wise son: but he that sleepeth in harvest is a son that causeth shame."*
>
> Proverbs 11:30: *"The fruit of the righteous is a tree of life; and he that winneth souls is wise."*
>
> Matthew 9:37-38: *"Then saith he unto his disciples, the harvest truly is plenteous, but the labourers are few; Pray ye therefore the Lord of the harvest, that he will send forth labourers into his harvest."*

Reverend Betty Haynie's passion for lost souls was coupled with her perseverance and tenacity. This was a woman who had suffered personal losses in her own life, yet she pursued the purpose and calling of God. As a teenager, she had lost her sister to cancer. She reared her sister's three children almost singlehandedly and continued to blaze the trail, evangelizing and ministering to the brokenhearted and the oppressed. Despite her weariness or her struggles, she rallied up the energy to continue moving forward.

I took the time to detail Evangelist Haynie's character because her character traits impacted her ability to grow and develop followers—part of that was her ability to make the connection.

Generational and social gaps did not stop her from being human enough to reach across the table and impart truth and wisdom into our lives.

It is important to note that this group of young people from the summer of 1981 could have decided to leave. As most children do, they could have chosen to enjoy summer festivities and begin their summer vacation. However, they did not. They decided to follow Evangelist Haynie because she exhibited the traits of a spiritual mother. When spiritually appropriately nurtured, this generation, like the group in 1981, will choose spiritual progress over fleeting pleasures.

Evangelist Haynie is still imparting spiritual truth into the lives of young people even today. A couple of years ago, I was asked to speak at a conference in Florida where she was present. When I finished speaking, she walked up to me and said, *"You have such a pure heart."* Though simple, those words were very encouraging coming from her. I knew what she meant by those words. She had seen me at my worst but never gave up on me and never doubted that God would prove His Word in my life.

Evangelist Haynie's role in many lives is reminiscent of that of Naomi and Ruth in the Bible. Naomi was married and had two sons, who married two Moabite women, Ruth and Orpah. Tragedy struck their family. Not only did Naomi lose her husband Elimelech, whose name meant "king," but she also lost her two sons, Mahlon and Chilion—their names meant 'sickly' and 'pining' respectively

(Ruth 1:1-5).

Can you imagine the devastation of losing all of the men in your life at one time? Naomi was left with two daughters-in-law living in a foreign land. Her hopes and dreams of having grandchildren and living to a ripe old age caring for them had been dashed. The bitterness of spirit became so great until she was willing to forsake her birth name Naomi, which meant 'pleasant,' and choose to take on the name Mara which means 'bitterness.' Naomi's sorrow caused her entire perspective on life to change. She went from joyful and pleasant to bitter and despondent.

Naomi decided to journey back to Bethlehem to her people. What is so eye-opening about Naomi's decision to return home is that both of her daughters-in-law chose to follow her. Naomi had impacted these young women's lives to the extent that they were willing to leave the familiar for the unfamiliar, the known for the unknown. Naomi encouraged her daughters-in-law to go back to their people in hopes that they could find husbands and bear children by returning to their people. Orpah decided to return to her people, but Ruth made allegiance with Naomi and refused to leave her side.

> Ruth 1:16-17 *"And Ruth said, Intreat me not to leave thee, or to return from following after thee: for whither thou goest, I will go; and where thou lodgest, I will lodge: thy people shall be my people, and thy God my God. Where thou diest, will I die, and there will I be buried: The Lord do so to me, and more also, if ought but death part thee and me."*

Naomi had made such an impression on Ruth's life that she was willing to cling to her mother-in-law even until death. Naomi had made the connection that only a spiritual parent can have on a child. Just as Evangelist Betty Haynie had crossed over generations, Naomi made a similar connection. For both Naomi and Ruth, the relationship paid dividends in their future.

As the story continues, Naomi being a wise woman, understood that Ruth is a woman of marrying age would have desires for companionship. Naomi guides Ruth in the securing of the next kinsman for a husband. Ruth would eventually become the wife of a wealthy landowner, Boaz.

As the story unfolds, Ruth becomes the mother of Obed Edom, the father of Jesse, the father of King David. As legacy would have it, this would become the lineage of Jesus, our Savior, and King. Naomi had lost her husband Elimelech, whose name meant king, but our Father's eternal King never left her uncovered and unprotected. God was ever directing her course.

In the end, the daughter-in-law that Naomi had nurtured as her daughter became better to her than seven sons by the birth of Obed. The sorrow and bitterness of Naomi's pain had been turned to joy, praise, and promise. This is the blessing that comes when spiritual parents make the connection with spiritual children. God turns our sorrows into laughter.

Ruth 4:14-17: "*And the women said unto Naomi, blessed be the*

Lord, which hath not left thee this day without a kinsman, that his name may be famous in Israel. And he shall be unto thee a restorer of thy life, and a nourisher of thine old age: for thy daughter in law, which loveth thee, which is better to thee than seven sons, hath born him. And Naomi took the child, and laid it in her bosom, and became nurse unto it. And the women her neighbors gave it a name, saying, there is a son born to Naomi; and they called his name Obed: he is the father of Jesse, the father of David."

Spiritual fathers and mothers, as well as the spiritual children that they nurture, can benefit from the symbiotic relationship. Spiritual parents experience the joy of seeing their spiritual children develop into impactful leaders. In turn, spiritual children gain from the wisdom amassed by their spiritual parents through the years.

Not Many Fathers is all about making the connection. These are the ten principles that will help spiritual parents make that kind of connection:

1. We must see beyond our insecurities and recognize that there is a demand for spiritual parents in this hour.
2. We must remember that there were spiritual parents in the past who made indelible marks on our own lives; now, we must, in turn, pass it on.
3. We must resolve all the underlying issues in our personal lives that will hinder us from being models to the spiritual children of today.

4. We must be resolute in our pursuit to make spiritual connections wherever we are.
5. We must reinvest ourselves in others.
6. When we feel that situations are beyond our reach and capabilities, we must be transparent enough to refer cases to others who are more equipped to deal with the challenges.
7. We must be role models of everything we seek to teach to others.
8. For every person whose life you impact, take consolation in the fact that that is a spiritual son or daughter you are rescuing.
9. Respect the individuality of each person you reach.
10. Be willing to repeat the process of making the connection with spiritual children as often as you can.

References

ABC News. (2006, September 12). Facts On Foster Care in America. Retrieved from ABC News: www.abcnews.go.com

Aksu, Lara (2020). Greatest Women in History. The Journal of Students.

American SPCC. (2021). National Sexual Assault Online. Retrieved from amsericanspcc.org.

Alia, A. K. (2010). Assessing the Impact of Paternal Involvement on Racial/Ethnicity. Journal of Community Health.

Benson, Joseph. "Commentary on 2 Samuel 14". Joseph Benson's Commentary. https://www.studylight.org/commentaries/eng/rbc/2-samuel-14.html. 1857.

Blankenhorn, David. (1995). Fatherless America: Confronting Our Most Urgent Social Problem. New York: Basic.

Britannica, The Editors of Encyclopedia. "Baal." Encyclopedia Britannica, 23 Jan. 2020, https://www.britannica.com/topic/Baal-ancient-deity. Accessed 18 June 2021.

Brown, R. J.-A.-D. (1871). The First Epistle of Paul the Apostle to the Corinthians. Blue Letter Bible.

Bureau, U. S. (2020). The Proof is in Father Absence Harms Children. Retrieved from National Fatherhood Initiative: www.Fatherhood.org

Cruden, A. (1737). Cruden's Complete Concordance of the Old Testament and the New Testament. Grand Rapids Michigan: Zondervan.

DSM-5. (2013). Diagnostic and Statistical; Manual of Mental Disorders. Arlington, Va.: American Psychiatric Association fifth edition.

Edward Kruk, P. (2012). Father Absence, Father Deficit, Father Hinge "The Importance of Paternal Presence in Children's Lives. Psychology Today.

Encyclopedia of Children's Health. (n.d.). Retrieved from Health of Children: http://www.healthofchildren.com/

Fuller, J. (2020). 10 Reasons Why Pastors Leave the Ministry: https://www.pastoralcareinc.com/articles/10-reasons-why-ministers-quit/

Gates, M. F. (2003, October 16). Powerful Voices Annual Luncheon. Retrieved from Gates Foundation: www.gatesfoundation.org

Grace Y. Lee, B. S. (2014, January). Fetuses Respond to Father's Voice but Prefer Mother's Voice. Developmental Psychobiology, 1000.

Guzik, D. (2018). 1 Timothy 3. Retrieved from Enduring Word Commentary: www.EnduringWord.comGuzik, D. (2018). 2 Kings 13. Retrieved from Enduring Word:

www.EnduringWord.com/biblecommentary2kings/

Haddrick, M. (2018, March 29). 12 of The Most Famous Women in History. Retrieved from Biography: www.biography.com

Hailey Branson-Potts, E. M. (2020, February 24). Vanessa Bryant's Tribute to Kobe, the father, the husband, bring Tears and Smiles. Retrieved from Los Angeles Times: www.LATimes.com

Harmon, K. (2010, May 6). How Important is Physical Contact with Your Infant? Retrieved from Scientific American: https://www.scientificamerican.com/

Henry, Matthew. (1997). Matthew Henry's Concise Commentary On the Whole Bible. Nashville: Nelson.

Hill, N. (n.d.). Retrieved from Brainy quote: www.brainyquote.com

Holy Bible, New International Version®, NIV® Copyright ©1973, 1978, 1984, 2011 by Biblica, Inc.® Used by permission. All rights reserved worldwide.

Ingrahm, C. (2019, February 6). People like the estate tax a whole lot more when they learn how wealth is distributed: Most Americans Inherit Wealth. Retrieved from Washington Post: https://www.washingtonpost.com/

Ingrahm, C. (n.d.). People Like the estate tax a whole lot more when they learn how wealth is distributed. Retrieved from Washington Post.

Israel. (n.d.). Retrieved from En.wikipedia.org/wiki/Israel

Stonestreet, J., & Rivera, R. (2019, August 28). The Declining Respect for Clergy. Retrieved from Christian Post: https://www.christianpost.com/voices/the-declining-respect-for-clergy.html Kail, J. (2015, June 20). 4 Characteristics of Spiritual Fathers. Lancaster: https://jakekail.com/4-characteristics-spiritual-fathers/

Kenneth L. Baker, g. (2002). New International Study Bible. Grand rapids: Zondervan.

King James Version (1998). The Holy Bible. Nashville: Holman Bible Publishers.

Leonard, J. (2020, February 20). What to Learn About Abandonment issues? Retrieved from Medical News Today: www.medicalnewstoday.com

Levine, P. B. et al. "Roe v Wade, and American fertility." American Journal of Public Health. V0ol. 89, 2 (1999): 199-203. doi:10.2105/ajph.89.2.199

Maxwell, J. C. (1998). The 21 Irrefutable Laws of Leadership. Nashville: Thomas Nelson, Inc.

Maxwell, J. C. (2018). Developing The Leader Within You 2.0. Nashville: HarperCollins.

Moments in America: The State of America's Children in 2020. (2021). Retrieved from Children Defense Fund: https://www.childrensdefense.org/

Morris, L. (1985). First Corinthians: An Introduction and Commentary. Downers Grove:

Intervarsity Press.

Munn, G. L. (Fall, 1960). The Historical Background of First Corinthians. Southern Journal of Theology, Volume 3.

Nordlund, S. (2019, November 20). Ranking of Professions from most to least dishonest. Retrieved from Moneywise: www.moneywise.com

Oshinkale, Y. (2019, September 18). Definition of Mentorship: What is a Mentor? Retrieved from World Education Service: https://www.wes.org/advisor-blog/definition-of-mentorship/

Perry, T. (n.d.). Wikipedia. Retrieved from Daddy's Little Girls: wikipedia.org

Health, Vol. 89, No. 2.

Popenoe, D. D. (2011). The Significance of a Father's Influence. Retrieved from Focus On the Family: www.focusonthefamily.com

Raeburn, P. (2010). Daddy's Influence? The Surprising Connection between Fathers and their Offspring During Pregnancy. Today.

Resources That Inform and Equip Foster Parents. (2018, 11 3). Retrieved from A Fostered Life: www.afosteredlife.com

Root, A. (2010). The Children of Divorce. Grand Rapids: Baker Academic.

Russell, B. (2019, September 21). Why Do So Many Ministers Drop Out of Ministry? https://www.biblicalleadership.com/blogs/why-do-so-many-ministers-drop-out-of-ministry/

Shimron, Y. (2019, July 16). New Polls Show Growing View that Clergy Are Irrelevant. Retrieved from New Religion: www.Religionnews.com

Sheth S., Hoff, M., Ward, M., & Tyson, T. (2021). These 8 Charts Show the Glaring Gap Between Men's and Women's Salaries in the US. Retrieved from Insider: www.BusinessInsider.com

Statz, S. (2020). The Reasons Why Pastors Leave the Ministry. Retrieved from Fuller Institute, George Barna and Pastoral Care, Inc.: www.stevestutz.com

Strong, J. (1890). Strong's exhaustive concordance of the Bible. Chicago: Abingdon Press.

Szalavitz, M. (2010). Touching Empathy. Psychology Today.

Szalavitz, M. (2010). What Happens If You Don't Touch a Baby? Psychology Today.

The Holy Bible, English Standard Version. ESV® Text Edition: 2016. Copyright © 2001 by Crossway Bibles, a publishing ministry of Good News Publishers.

U.S. Census Bureau. (2020). Living arrangements of children under 18 years old: 1960 to present. Washington, D.C.: U.S. Census Bureau.

Wikipedia. (n.d.). Abortion in the United States. Retrieved from

Wikipedia: en.wikipedia.org/wiki/abortionintheUnitedStates

Wikipedia. (n.d.). Wikipedia. Retrieved from en.wikipedia.com

Williams, G. (2020, February 23). The New Dad's Voice Guide to Baby Bonding-Parenting. Retrieved from www.parenting.com

Wolff, E. (2011, January). Inheritances and Distribution of Wealth or Whatever. Retrieved from U. S. Department of Labor: www.bls.gov

Wood, E. (2016, November 22). 5 Traits to Look for in a Mentor for your Child. Retrieved from First Tee: FirstTee.org

Young, A. (n.d.). Pinterest. Retrieved from Pinterest.com.

ABOUT THE AUTHOR

Dr. Jonathan Ramsey is a prolific preacher and teacher of the Gospel. He has over 40 years of Pastoral Leadership experience. He is a well sought after speaker who has had the privilege of preaching all over the world

Dr. Jonathan Ramsey, Jr. is a graduate of Lee University, Pentecostal Theological Seminary, where he received his Masters of Divinity and Masters in Counseling. He has an earned Doctorate of Philosophy from the European Theological Seminary.

Dr. Ramsey's most important role is as a family man. He is the loving husband to Lady LaVerne Ramsey and father to Ashley, Jonathan (Tamika), and Nathan. He serves as Lead Pastor of Rehoboth Church of God in Bloomfield, CT.

Made in the USA
Middletown, DE
21 June 2024

55718387R00117